No. [illegible]

County Examination Questions,

With Answers.

STATE OF KANSAS.

COUNTY

EXAMINATION QUESTIONS,

STATE OF KANSAS,

JANUARY, 1901, TO OCTOBER, 1901.

WITH ANSWERS.

No. 9.

TOPEKA, KAS.:
JOHN MACDONALD.
1902.

THE NEW YORK
PUBLIC LIBRARY
283397
1903

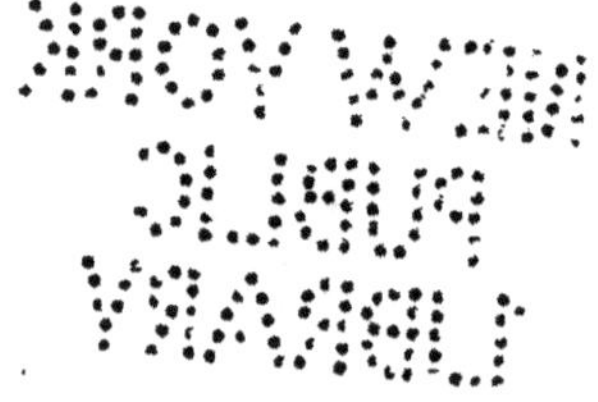

Index.

CORRECTIONS.

In answer to Question 1 in Constitution, page 110, instead of the phrase "Majority vote of the members elected in each house" wherever it occurs in the answer to question 1, the phrase "A majority vote of a quorum in each house" should be used.

In subdivisions (*b*) and (*c*) in answer 3, in Physics, page 170. substitute the following:

(*b*) amperage $= \frac{\text{voltage}}{\text{ohmage}} = \frac{1.1}{8+\frac{1}{3}} = .132$ amperes.

(*c*) Yes; the current would be stronger.

Questions for Examination.

January 26, 1901.

ARITHMETIC.

[Nichols.]

1. *Explain fully the process of division by fractions, and illustrate by an original problem.*

Ans. Let it be required to divide $\frac{3}{4}$ by $\frac{5}{8}$.
$1 \div \frac{5}{8} = \frac{8}{8} \div \frac{5}{8} = \frac{8}{5}$.
Since $1 \div \frac{5}{8} = \frac{8}{5}$, $\frac{3}{4} \div \frac{5}{8}$ must equal $\frac{3}{4} \times \frac{8}{5}$ or $\frac{6}{5}$.

Rule: To divide by a fraction, multiply the dividend by the reciprocal of the divisor, or, in other words, invert the terms of the divisor and proceed as in multiplication.

Problem: How many apples at $\frac{3}{4}$c. apiece can be bought for $7\frac{1}{2}$c.?

Solution: Since one apple costs $\frac{3}{4}$c., as many apples can be bought for $7\frac{1}{2}$c. as $\frac{3}{4}$c. is contained times in $7\frac{1}{2}$c., or 10 apples.

2. *Find the greatest common divisor of 36 and 200 by factoring.*

Ans. Solution:
36=2, 2, 3, 3.
200=2, 2, 2, 5, 5.
2×2=4, G. C. D.

3. *A can do a piece of work in 4 days, B in 6 days, C in 8 days, and D in $2\frac{3}{11}$ days. How much longer will it take A and C working together than B and D together to accomplish the work?*

Ans. A can do $\frac{1}{4}$ in one day.
C can do $\frac{1}{8}$ in one day.
Both can do $\frac{3}{8}$ in one day.
∴ It will take A and C $2\frac{2}{3}$ days.
B can do $\frac{1}{6}$ in one day.
D can do $\frac{11}{25}$ in one day.
Both can do $\frac{91}{150}$ in one day.
∴ It will take B and D $1\frac{59}{91}$ days.
Difference is $1\frac{5}{273}$ days.

4. *How much will it cost to excavate a cellar 12 by 15 feet and 6 feet deep, at 25 cents a cubic yard, and wall it with a stone wall 18 inches thick, at $1.50 a perch?*

Ans. Cost of excavation $= \frac{\$.25 \times 12 \times 15 \times 6}{27} = \$10.$

Cost of wall $= \frac{\$1.50 \times 48 \times 6}{16\frac{1}{2}} = \$26.18+$

Total cost $= \$36.18+$

Note: The masonry will make a wall 48 ft. long, 6 ft. high, and 1½ ft. thick. A perch is 16½ ft. long, 1 ft. high, and 1½ ft. wide. Hence the area of one side of this wall, divided by 16½, will give the number of perches.

Masons sometimes take the outer perimeter of the wall for the length. In this case the cost of the wall would be $29.45+

5. *If 4 men build a wall 60 feet long, 18 inches wide, and 3 feet high, in 6 days, how long will it take them to build a wall 40 feet long, 12 inches wide, and 4 feet high? Solve by compound proportion.*

Ans. $\left.\begin{matrix} 60 : 40 \\ 18 : 12 \\ 3 : 4 \end{matrix}\right\} :: 6 \text{ da.} : x$

$x = \frac{40,\ 12,\ 4,\ 6}{60,\ 18,\ 3} = 3\frac{5}{9}$ days.

6. *Extract the cube root of 29,791, explaining fully each step involved.*

Ans.

```
          29791(31
          27
          --------
  2700   |2791
    90   |
     1   |
  -----  |
  2791   |2791
```

"Analysis: Separate the number into periods of three figures each. Since there are two periods, the root will contain two figures. The first period considered as integral thousands is 29, the greatest cube of which is 3 tens, or 30. From the entire cube deduct the cube of the three tens = 27000, and there remains 2791, equal to $3t^2u + 3tu^2 + u^3$, &c." See Belfield's Arithmetic, page 279.

7. *Bought 1,000 bushels of corn at 16 cents a bushel. If the loss by shrinkage and waste is 5 per cent., for what*

must I sell per bushel to gain 12½ per cent. on my investment?

Ans. \$160 = cost of corn.
.125
\$20 = gain.
\$180 = selling price.
50 bu. was lost in shrinkage, hence 950 bu. must bring \$180.
Selling price per bu., \$$\frac{180}{950}$ = 18$\frac{18}{19}$c.

8. *Find difference between the simple and annual interest of \$650 for 2 years 6 months at 7 per cent.*

Ans. The simple interest is the interest on the principal only.
Interest on \$650 at 7% for 1 yr. is \$45.50.
Interest for 2½ years is 2½ × \$45.50, or \$113.75.
Annual interest is interest on the principal and on the unpaid annual interests, hence the difference between the simple and annual interest of the same principal for a given time at a given rate is the interest on the unpaid annual interests.
One year's interest, \$45.50, bears interest at 7% for 1 year and 6 months.
Also \$45.50 bears interest for 6 mos., or, \$45.50 bears interest for 2 years.
Difference = \$45.50 × .07 × 2 = \$6.37.

9. *Loaned \$500 at 8 per cent. and received in payment \$565. Find length of time money was loaned.*

Ans. Solution: \$65 = the interest.
\$40 = interest for 1 yr.
No. yrs. = $\frac{65}{40}$ = 1$\frac{5}{8}$.
∴ Time = 1 yr. 7 mo. 15 days.

10. *Which is the better investment, and how much—\$5,000 3-per cent. government bonds at 104½, or \$5,000 taxable stocks at par (taxed at 3 per cent. on one-half value), and yielding an income of 5 per cent?*

Ans. Cost of bonds = \$5225.
Income = \$150.
Rate of income = 2$\frac{182}{209}$%
Cost of stock = \$5000.
Income = \$250.
Tax = \$75.
Net income = \$175.
Rate of income = 3½%.
∴ The latter is $\frac{263}{418}$% better.

GRAMMAR.

[Bushey.]

"Rest is not quitting the busy career,
Rest is the fitting of one's self to one's sphere.
'Tis the brook's motion, clear without strife,
Fleeting to ocean after its life;
'Tis loving and serving the highest and best;
'Tis onward unswerving: and this is true rest."

1. *Give construction of* QUITTING, *line 1 of above passage.*

Ans. Quitting is a present, active participle used as the predicate of *is* after *rest.*

2. *Give construction of* MOTION, *line 3 of above passage.*

Ans. Is the predicate nominative of "it" after "is."

3. *Give construction of* FLEETING, *line 4 of above passage.*

Ans. Adjective modifying "brook."

4. *Give construction of* BEST, *line 5 of above passage.*

Ans. Adjective modifying "loving and serving."

5. *Give construction of* ONWARD, *line 6 of above passage.*

Ans. Predicate adjective of "it" after "is."

"It might, I think, be sufficient to object to this explanation that language would then be an accident, and, this being the case, that we should somewhere find tribes so low as not to possess it."

6. *Point out the principal clause in above sentence.*

Ans. I think.

7. *Give construction of the word* CASE (*line 10*).

Ans. The predicate-nominative of *this* after *being* in the participial-absolute expression, "this being the case."

8. *Give construction of* TO OBJECT (*line 7*).

Ans. To object is the subject of the sentence. *It* is an expletive or introductory word.

9. *Construct a sentence containing a copulative verb other than the verb* TO BE.

Ans. He *seems* a man. *To be* is the only pure copula.

10. *Construct a sentence containing a factitive object.*

Ans. They chose him *captain.*

GEOGRAPHY.

[Nelson.]

1. *What are the principal four products of South America?*

Ans. Coffee, hides, sugar, caoutchouc.

2. *Name and describe three of the most important rivers of the world.*

Ans. The Mississippi rises near the 50th parallel, north latitude, in North America, and flows generally south and southeast, east of the central part of the United States, 4,200 miles, into the Gulf of Mexico, draining a basin of 1,250,000 square miles. The Missouri is included as a part of the Mississippi.

The Amazon rises in the western part of South America, north of the center, flows generally east and northeast, 4,000 miles, and discharges into the South Atlantic ocean, draining an area of 2,500,000 square miles.

The Nile, rising near the equator in east-central Africa, flows generally north for 4,000 miles, and discharges into the Mediterranean after draining 1,400,000 square miles.

3. *Name countries bordering on the Mediterranean sea.*

Ans. Spain, France, Italy, Austria-Hungary, Montenegro, Turkey in Europe, Greece, Turkey in Asia, Egypt, Tripoli, Tunis, Algeria, Morocco.

4. *Tell in from ten to twenty lines the principal facts you would expect an advanced class in geography to know after a study of North America.*

Ans. Its size, form, location, comparative size; its coast line; the topographical features of the country; the length, size of basin, relative importance and value of its principal rivers; its lake systems, their size, peculiar characteristics and importance; its mountain systems, their location, trend, general features and importance; the distribution of its deserts, plains, plateaus and forest lands; its climate, the reasons for the varying climatic conditions; the description of its fauna and flora; its commercial importance; seaports; lines of navigation; cable communication; condition of foreign commerce; its internal commerce with means of communication and transportation; the value and location of the principal natural products; the value and location of the principal manufactured products; the industrial, commercial and agricultural life of its people; the character and civilization of its peoples, together with their location, number and distribution; its division into political states or communities and a general idea of the forms of government under which those people live.

5. ***Name principal mountains, rivers and lakes of the United States.***

Ans. Principal mountains, the Appalachian system on the east and the Rocky Mountain system on the west. The principal individual mountains are Mts. Whitney, Rainier, Shasta, Hood; and Peaks, Longs, Pike's and Frémont's in the Rockies, and Mts. Mitchell, Washington, Marcy and Katahdin in the Appalachian system.

The principal rivers are the Columbia, Sacramento, Colorado, Rio Grande, Mississippi, Alabama, Savannah, Potomac, Delaware, Hudson, Connecticut, and a portion of the St. Lawrence.

Its principal lakes are the Great Lake system, composed of lakes Superior, Michigan, Huron, Erie and Ontario, and numerous small lakes in contiguous States, the Great Salt Lake, the Klamath Lake system in Oregon and its extension across northeastern California into western Nevada, lakes Tulare in California, Flat Head in Montana, Coeur d'Alene in Idaho, and Chelan in Washington.

6. ***Draw a map of Kansas, indicating*** (a) ***natural features,*** (b) ***location of State institutions.***

[Cannot reproduce diagram.—Ed.]

7. ***Define zone, valley, peninsula, glacier, mountain system.***

Ans. (*a*) A belt of land and water lying between or within certain fixed but imaginary lines.

(*b*) A valley is a space of land inclosed between ranges of hills or mountains, or the depressed land lying alongside a river or watercourse.

(*c*) A portion of land almost surrounded by water.

(*d*) An immense mass of ice and snow which moves almost imperceptibly down the higher mountain valleys or slopes.

(*e*) Is a name given to several connected chains or ranges of mountains.

8. ***Locate the following: Arabian sea, Iceland, Rhone river, Puget sound, Atlanta, Stockholm, Danube river.***

Ans. (*a*) It is an indentation into the southwestern part of Asia, and touches upon Hindustan, Baluchistan, Persia, Oman, and Arabia.

(*b*) Iceland is an island lying between 66° north latitude and the Arctic Circle, and 12° west and 24° west longitude in the Atlantic ocean.

(*c*) The Rhone river flows through eastern and southeastern France and empties into the Mediterreanean.

(*d*) Puget Sound is in western Washington, and is connected with the Pacific ocean by means of the Strait of San Juan de Fuca and also with the Gulf of Georgia.

(*e*) Atlanta is northwest of the center, and is the capital of the State of Georgia.

(*f*) Stockholm, the capital of Sweden, lies on the east coast on the Baltic sea.

(*g*) The Danube rises in the German empire, flows generally east and southeast through the German empire, Austria-Hungary, forms a part of the boundary between Austria-Hungary and Servia, the boundary between Roumania and Servia, a part of the boundary between Roumania and Bulgaria, and, flowing through Bulgaria, discharges into the Black sea, after traveling 2,000 miles, and draining 200,000 square miles of territory.

UNITED STATES HISTORY.

[Riggs.]

1. *Why was Magellan's voyage regarded as of great importance?*

Ans. It proved that the earth is round; that South America is a great continent; that there is no short southwest passage to India.

2. *Give a sketch of the American enterprises of Sir Humphrey Gilbert and Sir Walter Raleigh.*

Ans. Queen Elizabeth granted to Sir Humphrey Gilbert any new land he might discover in America. He failed in his first attempt, and while on his way home, after landing in Newfoundland, his ship with all on board went down at sea. This occurred in 1583. The next year (in 1584), Sir Walter Raleigh, Gilbert's half-brother, obtained a permission from Queen Elizabeth to make a settlement in North America, and sent out an expedition. The explorers landed on Roanoke Island, off the coast of North Carolina, and told such marvelous stories about the land on their return that Elizabeth called it "Virginia," after herself; and Raleigh determined to plant a colony there. In 1585, 108 emigrants under Ralph Lane left England and built a town on Roanoke Island. They were unfitted for the task, and would have starved to death if Sir Francis Drake had not touched there and brought them home to England. But they brought with them the "Irish potato," and some dried tobacco leaves which the Indians had taught them to smoke. In 1587 Raleigh sent out a second colony, composed of both men and women. This colony was under the direction of John White, with instructions to build the City of Raleigh somewhere on the Chesapeake Bay. He landed on Roanoke Island, where, on the 18th day of August, 1587, was born his granddaughter, Virginia Dare, the first child born of English parents in America. Gov. White returned to England for supplies, was detained three years by the Spanish War, and when he came back every soul had perished. Raleigh had impoverished himself, and in 1589 made over all his rights to a joint-stock company of merchants. This ended his attempts to make a settlement in North America.

3. *What principles, then new, were made by Roger Williams a part of the law of the "Providence Plantations"?*

Ans. That church and state should be separated; all religious beliefs should be tolerated; all laws requiring attendance on religious worship should be repealed; the soil belonged to the Indians; the settlers could obtain a valid title only by purchase from the Indians; accepting a deed for the land from a mere intruder like the monarch of England was a sin requiring public repentance.

4. *Give an account of Braddock's defeat.*

Ans. Braddock took command of an expedition against the French, which was to go from Ft. Cumberland across Pennsylvania to Ft. Duquesne. He left Ft. Cumberland in June. The march was slow, but on July 9th, 1755, he had crossed the Monongahela river, and was but eight miles from the fort when his advance guard came face to face with an army of Indians and French. This army hid behind the trees and bushes, and from their ambush poured volley after volley into the British. The English soldiers would have been glad to fight in Indian fashion, from behind trees, as Washington, who was one of Braddock's aides, had advised, but Braddock thought this was cowardly, and made them stand up in line till so many were killed that he had to retreat. They would probably have been killed to a man if Washington and his Virginia troops had not covered their retreat. Braddock was wounded, and died a few days afterward.

5. *What was the "Gadsden Purchase," and why so called?*

Ans. When the attempt was made to run the boundary-line between the United States and Mexico from the Rio Grande to the Gila river, so much trouble was encountered that a new treaty was made with Mexico in 1853, establishing the present boundary from the Rio Grande to the Gulf of California. This line is far south of the Gila river, and for the additional tract of land, 45,535 square miles, the United States paid Mexico $10,000,000. It is called the Gadsden Purchase after James Gadsden, who negotiated the treaty.

6. *What were the "bogus statutes" of Kansas, and when were they repealed?*

Ans. They were statutes enacted by the Legislature at Shawnee Mission, Johnson county, in 1855, and were made in behalf of the Pro-Slavery party. These statutes were repealed at Lawrence, January, 1859.

7. *What was the character and the chief work of the Lecompton Convention?*

Ans. It was a Pro-Slavery convention, and its chief work was to frame a constitution which would bring Kansas into the Union as a slave State.

8. *Sketch the connection of John Brown with Kansas history.*

Ans. John Brown came to Kansas when border-ruffianism broke out here, in 1855. He came here with arms, and resisted the border ruffians with violence. He and his command committed some murders in retaliation for murders that had been committed by the ruffians; he was at last outlawed, and a price was set on his head. In 1858 he left Kansas, and in July, 1859, settled near Harper's Ferry, Va.

9. *Describe the encounter between the "Monitor" and the "Merrimac."*

Ans. March 8th, 1862, the "Virginia," which was the old United States schooner "Merrimac" transformed into an iron-clad, went out to destroy the wooden vessels of the United States Navy which were blockading Chesapeake Bay. She sank the "Cumberland" and burned the "Congress," and then returned to the shelter of the Confederate batteries. The next morning she came out to finish her work of destruction, and first attacked the "Minnesota," which was fast on a mud-bar. Before she could reach the "Minnesota" she was intercepted by a small iron hull on top of which rested a boat-shaped raft, covered with sheets of iron which formed the deck. On top of the deck, which was only three feet above the water, was an iron cylinder or turret carrying two guns and revolved by machinery. This vessel was called the "Monitor." Between these two ships occurred the greatest naval battle of modern times. When it ended, neither ship was disabled; but they proved that there was no further use for wooden ships on the sea. The "Virginia" or "Merrimac" withdrew from the fight, and a little later she was blown up, when Norfolk was surrendered to the Union forces. The "Monitor" sank in a storm off Cape Hatteras, in January, 1863.

10. *Give the circumstances connected with the assassination of Garfield.*

Ans. When President Garfield was inaugurated he incurred the enmity of Senator Conkling, of New York, by yielding to the recommendations of Mr. Blaine concerning certain New York appointments. Mr. Conkling and Mr. Platt, the other Senator from New York, resigned their seats in the United States Senate, and the Republican party broke into two factions: those supporting Mr. Conkling were called "Stalwarts" and those supporting President Garfield were called "Half-Breeds." The feeling grew so intense that a disappointed office-seeker named Charles J. Guiteau determined to remove the President. On the 2d day of July, 1881, as Mr. Garfield was about to take the train in the Baltimore & Ohio railway depot at Washington, Guiteau came up behind him and shot him in the back. After a long and painful illness the President died, Sept. 19th, 1881. Guiteau was tried, convicted, and hung.

READING.

[Massey.]

Now, little dolly, shut your eyes
  While mamma rocks you to sleep.
Dream of fairies and sunny skies,
  Until the little birds peep.

When you awake, my pretty one,
  The sun will be shining bright,
And we will play till set of sun,
  When we must say good-night.

—*Students' First Reader.*

Write ten questions on the poem such as you would ask

a class for the purpose of bringing the conscious experience of the children into the recitation.

Ans. (*a*) Can your dolly shut her eyes, and did you ever see one that could?

(*b*) Who is the dolly's mamma that rocks her to sleep, and does the dolly really sleep?

(*c*) Did you ever see a fairy, and what did it look like?

(*d*) What other kinds of skies are there besides sunny skies? What kind of a sky is it to-day?

(*e*) How do little birds peep? Did you ever hear them peep?

(*f*) How long does the dolly's mamma tell her to sleep? Do you sleep that long?

(*g*) How long does the dolly's mamma tell her to play? Do you ever play that long?

(*h*) Did you ever see the sun set? Tell us how it looks.

(*i*) Can your dolly go to sleep and dream? Can she play as you do?

(*j*) Can she speak, and if she can did she ever tell you good-night?

ORTHOGRAPHY.

[Riggs.]

1. *Define* VOCAL, SUBVOCAL, ASPIRATE, ACCENT *and* EMPHASIS. *Illustrate each by an example.*

Ans. (*a*) A purely vocal element of speech unmodified except by resonance; as, *a*.

(*b*) A speech element consisting of tones, not pure as in the vowels, but modified by some kind of obstruction in the oral or nasal passage, and in some cases with a mixture of breath sound; *b*.

(*c*) A sound consisting of or characterized by a breath, like the sound of h; *h*.

(*d*) A superior force of voice or of articulative effort upon some particular syllable of a word, distinguishing it from the others.

(*e*) A particular stress of utterance given in reading or speaking, to one or more words, whose signification the speaker intends to impress specially upon his audience. "The province of *emphasis* is much more important than that of *accent*."

2. *Define* SYLLABLE, ULTIMATE, PENULT, *and* ANTE-PENULT, *and give examples.*

Ans. (*a*) An elementary sound or a combination of elementary sounds uttered together, or with a single impulse of the voice, and constituting a word or a part of a word; *syl*, in syllable.

(*b*) The last or final syllable in a word; as *mate*, in ultimate.

(*c*) The syllable preceding the final syllable; as, *pe*, in penult.

(*d*) The syllable preceding the penult; as, *te*, in antepenult.

3. *Discriminate between the meanings of the words in each of these groups: gamble, gambol; peer, pier; auger, augur; principal, principle; core, corps, dying, dyeing; rain, rein, reign; cent, sent, scent; meat, meet, mete; cite, sight, site.*

Ans. (*a*) Gamble, to play or game for money or other stake; gambol, to dance and skip about in sport, to frolic.

(*b*) Peer, one of the same rank, an equal, a match, a mate; pier, any additional mass of masonry used to stiffen a wall, or, a projecting wharf or landing-place.

(*c*) Auger, an instrument for boring or perforating soils, rocks, woods or other materials; augur, to conjecture from signs or omens, to predict, foretell.

(*d*) Principal, highest in rank, authority, character, importance, or degree; the chief or main; principle, a fundamental truth.

(*e*) Core, the heart or inner part of a thing; corps, a body of men.

(*f*) Dying, the act of passing from life to death; dyeing, the process or art of fixing colors in fibrous materials.

(*g*) Rain, water falling in drops from clouds; rein, a portion of harness; reign, dominion or rule.

(*h*) Cent, 100th part of a dollar; sent, dispatched; scent, an odor.

(*i*) Meat, flesh of animals; meet, coming together from different directions; mete, a measure, limit or boundary.

(*k*) Cite, to summon with authority, to quote; sight, the act of seeing; site, situation, place or position of anything.

4. *Write the following words, indicating the pronunciation of each and the sound of each letter: squirrel, lecture, thyme, ghost, bush, drunk, cigar, amuse, loathe, gneiss. Explain your diacritical marks.*

[See dictionary.—Ed.]

5. *Spell correctly the following words: cushon, hauty, knau, Wensday, sirloin, bycicle, tunnel, nickel, monies, inviolet, marriageable, govenor, preferrable, rumatism, brakesman, pardner, musketo, mustache, fourty, postcript.*

(See any dictionary.—Ed.)

PENMANSHIP.

[Taylor.]

1. *What is the relation of motor control to penmanship?*

Ans. Penmanship is the result of muscular action; hence it is good or poor penmanship as the movements are or are not controlled in the execution of correct forms. This is a feature in learning to write, that should receive more thought and attention on the part of teachers. Correct motor control can be acquired only by individual effort; hence a course of graded lessons in writing should be mastered, one by one, by each pupil, in order that motor control may be in harmony with good writing.

2. *What class of movements are essential to easy, graceful writing?*

Ans. Muscular movement is essential to easy, graceful writing.

3. *Explain how you would instruct beginners to write.*

Ans. For mere beginners, five or six years old, I would write easy letters or words on the board several times, requiring them to watch me; then I would have them write the same about the same number of times; then I would write again, and have them write again. I would do this until the majority could write the exercise so it could be read by anyone. I would continue this method, increasing the words in length and difficulty of execution, until the children could write their reading lessons and language lessons. I would not require them to learn by mastering the forms of letters and writing them accurately until they were seven or eight years old.

4. *How would you overcome slovenliness in writing?*

Ans. By requiring each pupil to write the exercises, one at a time, and approving the work of each pupil on each exercise when the form and appearance of the page-work is satisfactory to myself. In this way neatness soon becomes a habit, and it often occurs that the most slovenly writers become the most careful writers.

5. *How is penmanship related to orthography?*

Ans. Penmanship and orthography are very closely related, since neither is ever used without the other. Good spelling helps the writing and good writing helps the spelling. The more legible the style of writing, the more it helps in spelling. The spelling-lesson should always be considered a special writing exercise, and each pupil should be required to write the spelling as well as he is known to be able to write at the special writing periods.

6. *Write a few lines indorsing a friend's character.*

[For the applicant.]

THEORY AND PRACTICE.

ELEMENTARY EDUCATIONAL PSYCHOLOGY.

[Taylor.]

1. *Name and define the various intellectual activities.*

Ans. Consciousness is self knowing its own states or activities.

Apperception is the mind recognizing elements in an experience as similar to those in a previous experience, and immediately giving the new experience the same meaning as the old.

Attention is the concentration of the mind upon some particular element in an experience.

Perception is the act of getting knowledge of individual objects present to the senses.

Memory is the act of recalling the picture of a past experience.

Imagination is the function which embodies the ideal in concrete form.

Conception is the creation of an image which symbolizes the general processes by which all the individual members of the class to which it belongs are constructed.

Judgment is the function which establishes the relation between ideas. It is the finding of the universal in the individual.

Reasoning establishes the relations between judgments. It is the operation by which the relations of certain things are found through the medium of others.

Some would include among the intellectual activities:

The Sensibilities, or the power of self to suffer pleasure or pain in the presence of joy or sorrow. The sensibilities are the motive power which excite to action.

The Will, which is the function by which the mind chooses, determines and acts.

2. *What are the relations of sensations to knowledge?*

Ans. The sensations are the only avenues through which the mind comes in contact with the outside world, hence they are the only means by which the mind can supply itself with the materials for knowledge.

3. *What kinds of ideas are derived from* (a) *sight?* (b) *touch?*

Ans. (*a*) Color, size, distance, light and shade, form. (*b*) Form, size, hardness, softness, smoothness, roughness, temperature, weight.

From both these senses in a modified degree comes the knowledge of proportions.

4. *What are the conditions of a ready memory?*

Ans. Memory acts readily and quickly in proportion as the understanding is clear, as the thing to be remembered affects personal interests and needs; as the original impression is vivid; as the thing to be remembered is definitely related to other knowledge; as the mind has followed a natural sequence in approaching the thing to be remembered.

5. *How are concepts formed?*

Ans. In four processes: Attention to one particular element, found common to all the individuals or members of the class; the comparison of the element thus discovered in the individual members of the class, and of other classes, and the verification of identity and differences; the gradual separation of the common element from the individuals in the class and its formation in the mind as a pure abstract mental image; the union or synthesis of all the elements found common to all the individuals in the class into one whole. This last process is the conception proper.

6. *What relations do concepts bear to the reasoning process?*

Ans. The judgment determines the relation between ideas or concepts. The reason establishes the relation between judgments; thus, the formation of a concept is the initial act of reasoning.

7. *Name and define the various classes of feelings.*

Ans. Feelings are divided into special sensations, general sensations, and emotions. Examples of the first class are sight, hearing, taste, smell, and touch. Of the second class are weariness, hunger, thirst, fatigue, temperature. In the third class are love, hate, grief, joy, ambition, etc.

8. *In what way are feelings developed?*

Ans. Special sensations are developed by experience and careful training along particular lines. The second class come as a result of the vegetative needs of the body, but are regulated to some extent by habit and experience. The emotions are developed by the most careful training at home and at school in supplying the child with the right ideals, and in securing the adherence of his self-activity to the realization of those ideals.

9. *Analyze will, and show its dependency upon the intellect and the feelings in general.*

Ans. Will is the function of the mind which chooses in the presence of desires, and having chosen the end to be reached, then selects the means to reach that end. That is, the will has two acts,—one idealizing, the other realizing. The idealizing act fixes the end. The realizing act chooses the means by which it gains that end. It is thus apparent that the will in idealizing depends upon the memory, imagination and other intellectual faculties, and in making its choice it is influenced and restricted by desires which have grown up through the education or mis-education of the sensibilities,—more especially by the dictates of conscience.

10. *How are you to profit by above knowledge?*

Ans. By putting into execution in the daily work of the school-room methods which will secure the systematic, orderly and natural development of all the faculties of the body, mind, will, and sensibilities.

THEORY AND PRACTICE.

GENERAL PEDAGOGICS AND METHODS.

[Taylor.]

1. *What knowledge on the part of the teacher do these subjects presuppose?*

Ans. A knowledge of the laws of the mind and of its development, together with a familiarity with the best methods of securing both orderly and systematic development. It also presupposes a mastery of the subjects in which the teacher assumes to give instruction.

2. *What is the relation of pedagogics to methods?*

Ans. Very nearly the relation of a science to an art. Pedagogics lays down the principles to be followed in teaching. Methods applies these principles in the daily work of the schools.

3. *Why does a knowledge of the latter only make an artisan rather an artist out of a teacher?*

Ans. Because without a knowledge of pedagogics the

teacher simply works as an automaton or a machine. With methods only, she works blindly without knowing *why* she does it.

4. *Define self-activity and explain methods of treating it.*

Ans. Self-activity is the self (child or man) reacting upon itself, which gives it the power to do the same thing again with more ease and rapidity than before. It may be treated as if self were made up of independent parts and while one of these parts is acting the others are still or at rest. The more modern view, however, seems to be that the self acts as a unit in all cases.

5. *Show the relation of the analytic and synthetic processes.*

Ans. The analytic and synthetic processes are like the two halves of an apple,—they are both necessary to produce understanding, a conception of the whole. The mind first analyzes; that is, resolves into parts. It then synthesizes by putting these parts together to make the whole.

6. *What defects in your own education are you able to correct in your pupils? Why?*

Ans. Defects in observation and in abstract reasoning. Because the mature mind has ascertained its own shortcomings, and it is more ready to detect and correct the deficiencies under which it labored.

7. *Outline the means you use in governing your pupils.*

Ans. Attempt is made to secure respect for the teacher and her authority, the child's respect for himself, an *esprit de corps* in the school. As far as possible every punishment appeals to each of these elements, and then the punishment follows swiftly and surely upon the commission of an offense. In its administration a calm and judicious impartiality is observed.

8. *Why do you regard them better than others generally used?*

Ans. Because generally, means employed do not appeal to the right element. Because punishment is dilatory and uncertain; and finally, because it is administered in a spirit of rage, revenge, or petulance.

9. *What are the characteristics of an ideal school?*

Ans. A school in which cheerfulness, obedience and industry on the part of the pupils are always present, and in which the teacher exercises a firm but gentle authority, without any visible signs of its existence.

10. *How would you increase the imaginative powers of your pupils?*

Ans. By encouraging them to write stories about their own experiences, about pictures which have been presented to them for their examination; about anecdotes or narratives related by others; and about historical events or happenings.

PHYSIOLOGY.

[Snow.]

1. *What are the effects of alcohol on the circulation?*

Ans. It absorbs the water from the blood; interrupts the interchange of substances in the capillaries; arrests oxidization throughout the body; reduces the temperature of the blood; deteriorates its quality and sets up diseased conditions; starves the tissues of the body; causes the blood to lose the power of coagulation; induces paralysis of the vaso-motor nerves, causing congestion in the capillaries; exhausts or weakens the heart action, and finally causes changes in the muscular structure of the heart, sometimes inducing fatty-degeneration of that organ.

2. *Describe the structure and action of the heart.*

Ans. It is composed of involuntary muscular tissues which contract regularly at equal intervals of time. There are two layers of muscular fibers, the superficial, which run spirally around the heart, forming a figure 8. The deep layers are circular in form. It is divided into four chambers by muscular partitions. The two chambers on the right side are entirely separated from the two on the left by a muscular partition in which there is no opening. The upper chamber on each side is called the right and left auricle respectively. The lower chamber on each side is called the right and left ventricle, respectively. The right auricle and ventricle propel the blood to the lungs; the left auricle and ventricle propel it from the heart to the different parts of the body. The valve between the right auricle and right ventricle has three leaves and is called the tri-cuspid valve. The one between the left auricle and ventricle has two leaves, and is called the mitral valve. The walls of the left side of the heart are thicker and stronger than are those of the right side, because more force is required to drive the blood throughout the system than is needed to send it to the lungs. The heart is a pump, a part of whose action is simply mechanical. Its action consists of alternate contractions and dilations which are called the systole and diastole; properly, however, the latter is a pause between the movements.

First, the great veins which open into the heart fill up, then these veins contract and the auricles fill, then the auricles contract and the ventricles fill. Then the ventricles contract and the aorta and pulmonary arteries expand with the columns of blood thrown into them, the heart rolling or twisting in a slight degree from left to right. This rolling movement is due to the figure 8 arrangement of the muscles of the heart. As the ventricles become empty they lengthen out again, come to a position of rest, which makes the diastole. At the same time the heart turns back or untwists itself.

3. *What is a lymph, how is it formed, and what becomes of it?*

Ans. Lymph is a fluid which closely resembles the plasma of the blood. It is formed of some of the ingredients of the blood and some of the waste matter resulting from the constant wear of the tissues. It is carried by the lymphatic vessels into the thoracic duct, which empties into the great vein at the left side of the heart, from whence it is carried to the lungs for purification before entering the general circulation.

4. *What is the temperature of the body? Through what channels is heat given off from the body?*

Ans. (*a*) 98½ deg. Fahrenheit.

(*b*) Heat may be removed by contact with cold objects, by radiation from its surface, and in other ways; but its regulation depends mainly upon the perspiratory action of the skin and exhalation of watery vapor by the lungs.

5. *What are the principal foodstuffs or proximate principles, and which of them may be partly digested in the mouth?*

Ans. (*a*) Proteids or nitrogenous foods; fats or oils; amyloids or starches; minerals, as water, etc.

(*b*) Starches.

6. *What ferments are found in pancreatic juice and upon what foods do they act?*

Ans. There are four ferments in pancreatic juice. One similar to pepsin, but acts only in an alkaline medium and completes the digestion of the proteids. The second ferment acts like saliva upon starch. The third operates in two ways upon the fats: it emulsifies them, and chemically decomposes them into fat acids and glycerine. These free acids then unite with the alkaline substances present and form soaps. The fourth ferment curdles milk.

7. *What are the functions of the skin?*

Ans. It envelops and protects the inner soft parts, and especially the ends of the nerves. It is one of the three principal organs of excretion. It regulates the temperature of the body; carries on a small amount of respiration, and adds to the ornamentation of the body.

8. *What are the cranial nerves? Name them.*

Ans. (*a*) They are the nerves which arise in twelve pairs from the under-surface of the brain, and, passing through openings in the cranial bones, are distributed to the organs of smell, sight, mastication, hearing, breathing, taste, digestion, circulation, and supply the face, eye, tongue, pharynx, and the muscles of the neck, chest and head with power of motion.

(*b*) Olfactory, optic, oculo-motor, trochlear, trigeminal, abducens, facial, auditory, glosso-pharyngeal, pneumogastric, spinal-accessory, hypo-glossal.

9. *How can the eye be accommodated normally for near and far objects?*

Ans. By the action of the ciliary muscles, which accommodate the eye for different distances by altering the shape of the crystalline lens.

10. *Of what use are the villi? cilia in trachea? Where are the cecum? omentum? patella peritoneum?*

Ans. (*a*) They are the absorbent vessels which cover the valvulæ in the small intestines. They lift the digested food from the intestine and pass it on into the blood vessels and lacteals.

(*b*) By their constant motion they drive out the mucus which is constantly secreted, and along with it the dust brought into the passage with the air.

(*c*) It is one of the three parts of the large intestine. It is a large sac on the right side which receives the contents of the small intestine.

(*d*) It is a fold of the peritoneum from the lower side of the stomach and spreading over the rest of the abdomen.

(*e*) The knee-cap, or chestnut-shaped bone, which acts as a shield to the knee-joint.

(*f*) A sac-like membrane which envelops the stomach and other organs situated in the abdomen.

CIVIL GOVERNMENT.

[Massey.]

1. *Name five weak points in the Articles of Confederation that have been strengthened by the Constitution.*

Ans. No executive head; no power in the Legislature to tax; no power in the Legislature to regulate trade; no judiciary; representatives dependent upon individual States for support.

2. *Discuss any one of the three great compromises of the Constitutional Convention.*

Ans. The compromise on representation. The populous States insisted that the number of representatives sent to Congress should be in proportion to the population of the State. The small States demanded that each State should send the same number of representatives. The compromise, which now exists, *i. e.*, equal representation in the Senate and unequal representation based on population in the House, was suggested by Connecticut.

3. *If a vacancy in the Senatorial representation of Kansas should occur* NOW, *how would it be filled?*

Ans. The Legislature, being in session, would elect. If the Legislature were not in session, the Governor would appoint.

4. *Name the present Lieutenant-Governor; Speaker of the House of Representatives of the State Legislature.*

Ans. (*a*) H. E. Richter, (*b*) George J. Barker.

5. *How does the United States compare with other nations in the training of men for the diplomatic service?*

Ans. The United States does not train its men for diplomatic service. It chooses its diplomats from the ranks of its public men, generally on account of political services.

6. *Distinguish clearly between the duties of an ambassador and a consul.*

Ans. An ambassador is the political and diplomatic representative of his government. He discusses with the foreign government all international matters; carries on all the preliminary correspondence and negotiation for the making of treaties and the settlement of international difficulties. The consul is the commercial representative of his government. He looks after the trade and commerce, and all imposts and duties between his government and that in which he is located. He also looks after the infraction of the minor rights of his fellow-citizens, and reports the more serious cases which he cannot adjust, to his minister or ambassador.

7. *Name five prohibitions on the States.*

Ans. No State shall enter into any treaty, alliance or confederation; grant letters of marque and reprisal; coin money; emit bills of credit; make anything but gold and silver coin a tender in payment of debts.

8. *Give five powers of Congress.*

Ans. To borrow money on the credit of the United States; to establish postoffices and post-roads; to declare war; grant letters of marque and reprisal, and make rules concerning captures on land and water; to raise and support armies; to provide and maintain a navy; to lay and collect taxes, duties, imposts and excises.

9. *Name the three departments of Government.*

Ans. Executive, legislative, judicial.

10. *What do you mean by civil service?*

Ans. The employment of clerks and other persons in the service of the Government of the United States independent of military and naval service, is called the civil service.

PHYSICS.

[Snow.]

Any eight of the ten.

1. *Distinguish between work and power, and define units for each.*

Ans. Work is the exertion of force through a distance. Power is the rate of doing work. The unit of work is the foot-pound, or the amount of work done when a weight of one pound is raised vertically to a distance of one foot. The unit of power is the foot-pound per second, or the expenditure of energy at the rate of one foot-pound each second.

2. *How far will a bullet shot horizontally with an initial velocity of 1,200 feet per second fall in the first 600 feet?*

Ans. A body will fall freely 16.08 feet in the first second. Suppose the initial velocity of 1,200 feet per second to be maintained during the first half-second of its flight, then it will have been a falling body for a half-second of time, which is approximately a fall of $\frac{8.04}{2} = 4.02$ feet.

3. *Explain the mercurial barometer and the siphon.*

Ans. (*a*) The mercurial barometer consists of a glass tube about thirty inches long, closed at one end, filled with mercury, inverted, with the open end dipped below the surface of mercury in a reservoir or cup. The column of mercury in the tube will fall in this latitude and altitude to between twenty-seven and thirty inches. If the atmosphere is lighter, the pressure on the surface of the reservoir which supports the mercury will be less and the column will fall. It the atmosphere be heavy, the pressure will be greater and the column will rise. The varying heights of the column will indicate the condition of the atmosphere, and thus forecast changes in weather.

(*b*) A siphon consists of a tube bent so that one arm is longer than the other. When the shorter arm is plunged below a water-surface and the tube exhausted of air, the pressure of air on the water surface will cause the water to rise through the height of the short arm and flow out through the long arm.

The principle in the barometer and the siphon is the same, namely, unbalanced pressures.

4. *State Boyle's law for gases, and explain its meaning.*

Ans. (*a*) At the same temperature the volume occupied by a given bulk of gas is inversely proportional to the pressure it supports..

(*b*) Suppose that a certain quantity of air at the ordinary pressure of the atmosphere occupies a volume of one quart. Then if the pressure on this quantity of air be increased to two atmospheres its volume will be reduced to one-half a quart, but if the pressure be reduced to one-half an atmosphere, the tension of the air will cause it to expand to two quarts. If the pressure be increased to 100 atmospheres, its volume will be decreased to one 1-100 of a quart. If the pressure of the atmosphere be reduced to one 1-100, then the volume of the air will be one hundred quarts.

5. *What is meant by the "dew-point"? by "relative humidity" of the atmosphere?*

Ans. The temperature at which air saturated with moisture deposits that moisture, is called the dew-point. The moisture of the air compared with air at the point of saturation is relative humidity.

6. *One pound of steam at 100°C. is condensed in twenty*

pounds of water at 10° and the resulting temperature is 40°; calculate the latent heat of vaporization of water.

Ans. The pound of steam raises 20 lbs. of water through 30°. If it had been condensed in 1 lb. of water it would have raised it through 20 × 30°, or 600°. But the steam in doing it would have lost but 60° of appreciable heat, hence the remainder, 540°, must have been derived from the latent heat of vaporization of water.

7. *How much current (amperes) will four cells of two volts and three ohms each send through an external resistance of fifty ohms, the cells being connected in series?*

Ans. A. equals amperage.
V. equals voltage.
O. equals ohmage.
R. equals outside resistance.
r. equals inside resistance.

Ohm's Law:

$$A = \frac{(4 \times 2) \text{ or } V.}{((4 \times 3) + 50) \text{ or } r. + R.}$$

$$A = \tfrac{8}{62}$$

8. *Why does a pond of water appear shallower than it really is?*

Ans. Because the effect of refraction in passing from the denser medium, water, to the rarer medium, air, is to bend the ray of light *from* the perpendicular. This causes the bottom of the pond to seem to be lifted up and brought nearer the surface.

9. *What is a continuous spectrum, and how can it be produced?*

Ans. (*a*) One uninterrupted by Fraunhofer's or dark lines.

(*b*) By producing the light so that it does not have to pass through surrounding masses of gases and vapors.

10. *To what are the dark lines of the solar spectrum due? Explain.*

Ans. (*a*) To selective absorption.

(*b*) The central body of the sun gives a continuous spectrum, but while the light is passing through the surrounding masses of gases and vapors, that light which is of the same color as the light which these gases emit is stopped or absorbed, and thus the dark lines are formed.

BOOKKEEPING.

[Bushey.]

F. H. Dawson opens retail dry-goods, January 1, 1901, with the following resources: Merchandise, $5,000; cash, $500.

Liabilities: Bills payable, $400.

Sells goods to T. W. Nilson, $50. Receives cash, $25; balance on account.

Pays rent, $15.

The store burns, and he receives $4,800 insurance.

Find Dawson's present worth.

JOURNAL. January 1, 1901.

	Mdse	$5,000	
	Cash	500	
	Bills payable		$400
	F. W. Dawson, proprietor		5,100
	Cash	25	
	T. W. Nilson	25	
	Mdse		50
	Expense	15	
	Cash		15
	Cash	4,800	
	Mdse		4,800

LEDGER.

F. W. Dawson.

Jan.	1	Loss		$165	Jan.	1			$5,100
Jan.	1	Present capital		4,935	Jan.	1	Gain		
				$5,100					$5,100
					Jan.	1	Present capital		$4,935

Bills Payable.

					Jan.	1			$400

Merchandise.

Jan.	1			$5,000	Jan.	1			$50
					Jan.	1			4,800
					Jan.	1	Loss		150
				$5,000					$5,000

Cash.

Jan. Jan. Jan.	1 1 1			$500 25 4,800	Jan.	1			$15

Expense.

Jan.	1			$15	Jan.	1	Loss		$15

F. W. Nilson.

Jan.	1			$25					

Loss and Gain.

Jan. Jan.	1 1	Expense .... Mdse........		$15 150	Jan.	1	F.W. Dawson		$165
				$165					$165

April 27, 1901.

ARITHMETIC.*

[Nichols.]

1. *Find the sum of the following fractions and reduce the result to a decimal fraction:*

$$\frac{1}{3},\ \frac{3}{5},\ \frac{3}{4},\ \frac{11}{12},\ \frac{1}{8}.$$

Ans.

$\frac{1}{3}$	40
$\frac{3}{5}$	72
$\frac{3}{4}$	90
$\frac{11}{12}$	110
$\frac{1}{8}$	15
$2\frac{29}{40}$	$\frac{327}{120}$

$2\frac{29}{40} = 2.725$

2. *What sum of money put at interest for 2 years at 6% will yield $200 interest?*

Ans. Interest on $1 for 2 years is 12 cents.
Principal $= \$\frac{200}{.12} = \$1666\frac{2}{3}$.

3. *A man bought 3 bushels of peanuts at $1.50 per bushel. He lost 1 bushel; 1 peck and 2 quarts were burned in roasting. He sold the remainder at 5 cents per pint. Did he gain or lose, and what per cent.?*

Ans. Cost = $4.50.
1 bu., 2 pks., 6 qts. or 108 pts. = quantity sold.
Amt. received = 108 × 5c. or $5.40.
∴ The gain is 90c., or 20%.

4. *What will it cost to carpet a room 12 ft. by 16 ft. with carpeting 27 inches wide at $1.20 per yard?*

Ans. It will take 8 strips one way or 6 strips the other way. In both cases 32 yds. will be required. 32 × $1.20 = $38.40, cost.

NOTE.—The buyer must pay for full strips.

5. *If 10 men do a piece of work in 4 days, in how many days will 6 men do it?*

Ans. If 10 men do it in 4 days, 1 man will do it in 40 days, and 6 men will do it in $\frac{1}{6}$ of 40 days or $6\frac{2}{3}$ days.

6. *What easy method do you know for determining whether 2 is a factor of a given number? 3? 5? 9? By which of these numbers is 3705 divisible? Tell how you know it.*

Ans. Use rules for divisibility by 2, 3, 5, 9.
3705 is divisible by 3 and 5.
Rules: A number is divisible by 3 when the sum of its digits is divisible by 3.
A number is divisible by 5 when its last digit is 0 or 5.

7. *Find the interest on $5600 for 1 year, 5 months, and 15 days, at 8%.*

Ans. 6% method.

```
  .06
  .025
  .0025
$ .0875 = int. on $1 at 6% for 1 yr., 5 mos., 15 days.
   5600
  ------
   5250
  4375
  ------
 $490 00 = int. on the principal at 6%.
  163.33⅓ =  "    "   "        "     "  2%.
 --------
 $653.33⅓ =  "    "   "        "     "  8%.
```

8. *Find the difference between the true discount and the bank discount on $2000 due in one year, interest being at 6%.*

Ans. Bank discount = 6% of $2000 or $120.
Present worth $= \frac{\$2000}{1.06} = \$1886.79$
True discount = $ 113.21
Difference = $6.79.

NOTE.—Days of grace should not be used in a problem of this kind.

9. *Find, to three decimal places, the length of the side of a square field whose area is 1 acre.*

Ans.

```
        160(12.649+
        144
  246 | 1600
      | 1476
 2524 |  12400
      |  10096
25289 |   230400
      |   227601
      |     2799
```

∴ The length of 1 side = 12.649+ rods.

10. *Bought Kentucky bonds at 90, due in 30 years, drawing 8% interest; what is the per cent. of income?*

Ans. One share costs $90 and yields $8.

$\therefore$ The rate of income $= \frac{8}{90}$ or $8\frac{8}{9}$%.

GRAMMAR.

[Bushey.]

"And now, after the severe chastisement of war, if the general sense of the whole country shall come back to the acknowledgment of the original assumption that it is for the best interests of all the states to be united, as I trust it will, I can perceive no reason why, under such restoration, we may not enter upon a new career, exciting increased wonder in the Old World by grander achievements hereafter to be made, than any heretofore attained, by the peaceful and harmonious workings of our American institution of self-government."

1. *Point out the principal clause in above sentence.*

Ans. "I can perceive no reason."

2. *What does the clause,* "as I trust it will," *modify?*

Ans. The clause beginning with "if," in line 2, and terminating with the word "united," in line 5.

3. *What is the construction of the clause,* "that it is for the best interests of all the states to be united," *(lines 4 and 5).*

Ans. The clause is in apposition with "assumption." The connective "that" is merely introductory.

4. *Give the construction of* "now" *(line 1).*

Ans. The adverb "now" is used here as a connective particle to introduce the inference or explanation contained in the sentence, and is equivalent to "under present circumstances," "things being as they are," or "in conclusion." Some authorities call it an adverb modifying "can perceive."

5. *Give the construction of* "exciting" *(line 7).*

Ans. A participle used as an adjective, and modifying "we."

6. *Give the construction of the clause,* "than any heretofore attained."

Ans. Adverbial element modifying "grander."

7. *Select three adjectives from above sentence, each in a different degree of comparison.*

Ans. "Severe," in line 1, is in the positive degree; "grander," in line 3, comparative; "best," in line 4, superlative.

8. *What is the construction of* "to be united" *(line 5)?*

Ans. An infinitive not used as a noun, depending upon the noun "states," which it limits. Some authorities would supply "which are" and call "to be united" the predicate of "which" after "are."

9. *Give a synopsis of* "shall come" *(lines 2 and 3) in third person singular.*

Ans. Indicative:

Pres., Comes. *Pres. Perf.*, Has come.
Past, Came. *Past Perf.*, Had come.
Future, Shall come. *Future Perf.*, Shall have come.

Subjunctive: The present is the only tense having a distinctive form — Come.

Potential:

Pres., May come. *Pres. Perf.*, May have come.
Past, Might come. *Past Perf.*, Might have come.

Imperative: Has no third person.
Infinitive: Always in third person.

10. *Construct a sentence containing an infinitive used to complete the meaning of a copulative verb.*

Ans. He seems *to enjoy* life.

[Omit any two questions.]

GEOGRAPHY.

[Nelson.]

1. *What and where are the following: Mediterranean, Amazon, Tokyo, Danube, Niger, Madagascar, Sydney, Ceylon, Korea, Himalaya?*

Ans. (*a*) A sea almost surrounded by Asia, Europe and Africa.

(*b*) A river draining equatorial South America, east of the Andes, discharging into the Atlantic.

(*c*) Capital city of Japan, on Hondo Island.

(*d*) A river draining central and southeastern Europe, discharging into the Black sea.

(*e*) A river draining the western portion of north equatorial Africa, and discharging into the Gulf of Guinea.

(*f*) An island off southeast Africa, in the Indian ocean.

(*g*) The capital city of New South Wales, Australia.

(*h*) An island in the Indian ocean, off the southeast coast of Hindustan.

(*i*) A peninsula between the Japan and Yellow seas, projecting from eastern Asia.

(*j*) The name applied to the high mountains lying between India and the Chinese empire.

2. *Define the following: Delta, glacier, zone, continent, equator, sea, hemisphere, island.*

Ans. (*a*) The silt brought down by the waters of a river settles near its mouth. Frequently the river divides into branches which cut their channels through this sediment. The lowlands thus formed are called the river's delta.

(*b*) Glacier is the name applied to a body of ice moving slowly down a mountain-slope, being forced along by the compact masses of the same substance farther up the slope.

(*c*) A belt of land and water lying between two parallels on the earth's surface.

(*d*) Is a name for a large body of land constituting a grand division of the earth's surface.

(*e*) An imaginary great circle passing around the earth midway between the two poles.

(*f*) The main bodies of water separating the continents are called *seas.*

(*g*) Half of the earth's sphere. Thus, we may have North and South Hemispheres, caused by the equator, or East and West Hemispheres, caused by a great meridian circle.

(*h*) A body of land entirely surrounded by water.

3. *Name six of the principal exports of the United States and tell to what countries they are sent; six of the principal imports, and state from what countries they come.*

Ans. (*a*) Corn, wheat, cotton, tobacco, iron and steel goods, and dressed meats. To England, Germany, India, France.

(*b*) Wines, silks, coffee, tea, beet sugar, jewelry. From France, Spain, Belgium, Germany, England, etc.

4. *Name and locate* (a) *important mountains in Europe and Asia;* (b) *important seas bordering upon Asia;* (c) *important islands along the coast of Europe.*

Ans. (*a*) *Europe:* Kiolen mountains, in the Scandinavian peninsula; the Alps, in central and western Europe; the Pyrenees, in Spain; the Apennines, in Italy; the Carpathians and Balkans in southeastern Europe; the Valdai Hills, in Russia; and the Ural and Caucasus, between Europe and Asia. *Asia:* The Taurus, in Asia Minor; the Kohrud, in Persia; the Eastern and Western Ghauts, in India; the Himalayas, between India and the Chinese empire; the Kuen-Lun, Thian-Shan, Nan-Shan, Khin-Gan, Nan-Ling, and Tayuling, in the Chinese empire; the Yablonoi and the Stanovoi, in Siberia.

(*b*) Okhotsk, Behring, Kara, Japan, Yellow, East China, South China, Arabian and Red seas, and the Bay of Bengal, Persian gulf, Gulf of Siam, and Gulf of Aden.

(*c*) British Isles, Lofoden Isles, Dagoe, Gotland, Danish Islands, Heligoland, Balearic, Corsica, Sardinia, Sicily, Ionia, Grecian Archipelago, Candia, Rhodes, Cyprus.

5. *What can you say of the natural sceneries of the United States, and what effect do they have upon our civilization?*

Ans. They embrace every variety, from the low alluvial plains of the semi-tropics to the lichen-bearing wastes of the frigid zones; from the fertile river valleys to the lofty mountains covered with perpetual snow; from narrow coast plain to the broad prairies, and even the desolate deserts. This of course makes for all kinds of industries,—mining, lumbering, agriculture, manufacturing and commerce,—and giving us all the elements of growth and power within ourselves, makes our civilization cosmopolitan and supreme, a world-embracing and world-building civilization.

6. (a) *Bound Kansas;* (b) *name and locate her State educational and charitable institutions.*

Ans. (*a*) North by Nebraska, east by Missouri, south by the Indian and Oklahoma Territories, and west by Colorado.

(*b*) Kansas State University, at Lawrence; State Normal School, at Emporia; Agricultural College, at Manhattan; Girls' Industrial School, at Beloit; Boys' Reform School, at Topeka; Men's Reformatory, at Hutchinson; School for Idiotic and Imbecile Youth, at Winfield; Institution for the Deaf and Dumb, at Olathe; Institution for the Blind, at Kansas City, Kansas; Soldiers' Orphans' Home, at Atchison; State Insame Asylums, at Topeka and Osawatomie, and a third one provided for.

7. *Name and locate the important rivers in North and South America, telling into what body of water each flows.*

Ans. (*a*) *North America:* Mackenzie, northern British Columbia, into the Arctic ocean; Yukon, Alaska, into Behring sea; Peace, west-central British Columbia, into Great Slave Lake; Saskatchewan, south-central British Columbia, into Hudson's bay; St. Lawrence, between Canada and United States, and through eastern Canada, into the Gulf of St. Lawrence; Connecticut, Hudson, Delaware, Susquehanna, and Potomac, all northeastern United States, into indentations of the Atlantic; James, Roanoke, Savannah, all eastern United States, into the Atlantic or its indentations; Appalachicola, Alabama, Sabine, Trinity and Brazos, all southern United States, into the Gulf of Mexico; Rio Grande, southwestern United States and boundary between the United States and Mexico, into the Gulf of Mexico; Colorado, southwestern United States, into the Gulf of California; San Joaquin and Sacramento, western United States, into the Pacific; Columbia, northwestern United States and southwestern British Columbia, into the Pacific; Humboldt, interior basin of United States, Rocky Mountain region, into Humboldt lake; the Mississippi-Missouri system, west-central, central and east-central United States, into the Gulf of Mexico.

(*b*) *South America:* Orinoco, northern, mainly in Venezuela, into the Atlantic; Magdalene, northern, in Columbia, into the Caribbean sea; Amazon, south equatorial region, mainly in Brazil, into the Atlantic; Sao Francisco, eastern, in Brazil, into the Atlantic; Rio de la Plata system, eastern and southeastern, into the Atlantic; Colorado and Negro, southeastern, into the Atlantic.

8. *Why are San Francisco, Kansas City, Chicago, New York, London, St. Petersburg, Melbourne, Rio Janeiro and Havana great commercial centers? Give causes for each.*

Ans. (*a*) Because it has such a fine harbor on the Pacific coast, and is the outlet for the coast country west of the Rockies.

(*b*) Because it is at the junction of the Kansas and Missouri rivers, and is the natural gateway for the prairie region south of Nebraska and north of Texas, as well as the southwest to Mexico.

(*c*) Because of its location upon the Great Lakes, and its proximity to the great wheat, corn and cattle regions of Illinois, Indiana, Iowa, Minnesota, and the Northwest as well as the West.

(*d*) For its excellent harbor, its location upon the Atlantic, and its age and consequent wealth.

(*e*) Because of its being the capital of England, its location upon a great navigable river, its age and wealth.

(*f*) The capital of Russia, and its location upon the only strip of external sea far enough south in the empire to encourage commerce and navigation.

(*g*) Its harbor, dividing as it does with Sidney, the command of the rich mining, grazing and agricultural wealth of Australia.

(*h*) Its harbor, and its command over the rich regions of Brazil.

(*i*) Its harbor, capital of Cuba.

UNITED STATES HISTORY.

[Riggs.]

1. *To what extent should Columbus be honored as the discoverer of America?*

Ans. As the man who first undertook to prove the rotundity of the earth and braved the dangers of an unknown sea against the protests and mutiny of his crew, and at last by his courage, energy and perseverance succeeded in blazing the way without which the continent would never have been discovered.

2. *Describe the attempts of the Huguenots to establish colonies.*

Ans. The first was that of John Ribault. In 1562 he built a fort in South Carolina, on a spot called Port Royal, and left it in charge of thirty men while he went back to France for reinforcements. The men left were shiftless, would not work, depended on the Indians till the Indians would feed them no longer, mutinied, slew their commander, built a crazy ship, put to sea, were found by an English ship and were taken in a famished condition and landed in London. In 1564 Laudonniere landed at the St. Johns river, in Florida, and built Fort Caroline, in honor of Charles IX. of France. Spain sent Menendez, who made a settlement at St. Augustine, in 1565. Ribault, who had returned, joined Laudonniere and attempted to attack the Spaniards, but a hurricane scattered his ships, and while it was still raging Menendez attacked Fort Caroline and massacred the men, women and children. A few days later Ribault with 149 men was driven ashore south of St. Augustine. Menendez came upon them, and massacred them also. For this a Frenchman named Gourgues, with three small ships and two hundred men, attacked St. Augustine, destroyed the fort, and killed every human being within it. Later Menendez, who was then in Spain, returned, and rebuilt St. Augustine.

3. *How did the cultivation of tobacco affect the growth of Virginia?*

Ans. It was the means of making Virginia the wealthiest, most populous and influential of the colonies,—a supremacy which continued long after the United States became a nation.

4. *What were the defects of the "Grand Model" of Locke, and how did it succeed?*

Ans. The Grand Model was too complicated a scheme of government for a new country. It established classes, when the conditions of life made it necessary that all men should be equal. It provided a large non-producing class, when it was absolutely necessary for the salvation of the colony that all should be producers. It was a miserable failure.

5. *Explain the "Monroe doctrine" and its application to recent history.*

Ans. (*a*) The Monroe doctrine was announced by President Monroe in his annual message to Congress, December 2, 1823. It announced that the American continents were not subject for future colonization by any European power; and declared further, that any attempt on the part of any government in Europe to extend its system to any portion of this hemisphere would be dangerous to our peace and safety, and that we, the United States, would regard any attempt to interfere with the independence that had been established by any country in North or South America, on the part of any European power, as the manifestation of an unfriendly spirit to the United States.

(*b*) In December, 1894, President Cleveland applied this doctrine to the dispute between Great Britain and Venezuela over a boundary-line, and forced Great Britain to submit the matter to arbitration. In 1898, while much was said about the Monroe doctrine, it was in no sense an excuse for our war with Spain.

6. *What question did the Civil War settle?*

Ans. The Civil War abolished slavery and destroyed the doctrine of States' rights, making the Federal Government a supreme sovereignty.

7. *Is universal suffrage, without regard to race, color, or sex, desirable? Justify your position.*

Ans. Yes, in the United States; because the suffrage has already been extended to men without regard to race, color or previous condition of servitude; and in order to make the Declaration of Independence a living truth and not a glittering generality, the same privilege ought to be extended to women. The question of race or color is not an open one, and cannot be considered.

8. *Into how many classes are American diplomatic agents divided, and what are included in each class?*

Ans. (*a*) Ambassadors extraordinary and plenipotentiary, including our representatives in France, Germany, Great Britain, Italy, Mexico, and Russia.

(*b*) Envoys extraordinary and ministers plenipotentiary. There are twenty-four of these, in countries ranging from Brazil and Spain to Portugal and Switzerland in importance.

(*c*) Ministers resident and consuls-general, four in number, at Corea, Liberia, Persia, and Siam.

(*d*) Consuls-general at such cities as Havana, Shanghai, and Vienna. There are twenty-eight of these cities, and, in addition to these, Santo Domingo.

(*e*) Secretaries of embassies and legation, who are stationed in the same countries with those of classes (*a*) and (*b*).

(*f*) Consuls at principal cities, sixty-one in number.

9. *Give the story of the "Virginius" affair in Cuba in 1873.*

Ans. During the Cuban insurrection, which began in 1868, an indignity to the American flag came near precipitating a war with Spain. On October 31st, 1873, the "Virginius," a ship floating the American flag, was captured on the high seas by a Spanish man-of-war, on the charge that she was bound for the island with men and arms for the insurgents. A number of persons were taken ashore and shot, without a trial, contrary to treaty and in spite of the protest of the American consul. Excitement ran high in the United States; war was imminent; but the difficulty was peaceably adjusted when it was shown that the "Virginius" had no right to fly our flag when captured, and when Spain had made all the reparation that was required by our government.

10. *Discuss briefly the Clayton-Bulwer treaty.*

Ans. The Clayton-Bulwer treaty, negotiated in 1850,

provided for a joint protectorate by the United States and Great Britain over the proposed canal across the State of Nicaragua; and both countries agreed not to occupy, fortify, colonize, assume or exercise any dominion over any part of Central America. This treaty marks the most serious mistake in our history, and has been condemned by Dr. Wharton, Secretary Blaine, President Buchanan, Secretary Cass, Secretary Foster, and other distinguished statesmen and diplomats. It is the only partial departure from the Monroe doctrine, for by it we recognize that England had something to say about the sovereignty of an American State.

READING.

[Massey.]

1. *Distinguish between accent and emphasis; force and pitch.*

Ans. (*a*) Accent is a particular stress of the voice laid upon some certain syllable of a word to distinguish it from other syllables.

Emphasis is stress of utterance given by a reader to a certain word or words to which he wishes to call the hearer's attention particularly.

(*b*) Force is the intensity of utterance, and pitch is the position upon the musical scale of the tone with which the word is uttered.

2. *Explain clearly the difference between thought interpretation and thought expression in reading.*

Ans. Thought interpretation is arriving at the understanding of the author's words; while thought expression is the giving that understanding to another.

3. *Define cadence, slur, rate, inflection, style.*

Ans. (*a*) The fall of the voice in reading or speaking, especially at the close of a sentence, or the rhythmical modulation of the voice.

(*b*) The indistinct pronunciation of words or syllables.

(*c*) The rapidity with which words or syllables are pronounced.

(*d*) The rising or falling slide or modulation of the voice.

(*e*) Refers to the character of the writing, as to whether it is narrative, didactic, etc.

4. *Name and define the different forms of voice.*

Ans. Effusive: In which the sound is emitted from the organs of speech in a calm or quiet way.

Expulsive: In which the words are forcibly uttered, as in animated description, declamation, and argumentation.

Explosive: In which the voice is projected from the vocal organs very rapidly and forcibly.

5. *Give a pedagogical reason for confining the first few reading lessons of a pupil to his ear vocabulary.*

Ans. To train the sense of hearing, to detect the differences in enunciation and pronunciation, and to train the vocal organs to enunciate and pronounce properly.

6 to 10. *Write ten questions, such as you would ask a fourth-reader class, about Whittier's "The Barefoot Boy."*

Ans. Point out the description and the apostrophe in the first stanza.

What knowledge does the barefoot boy gain that he never learns in school?

Why does Whittier call boyhood a time of June?

What are the riches of the barefoot boy?

What were the apples of Hesperides, and tell the story connected with them?

Why does Whittier ask the barefoot boy to live and laugh happily?

What kind of sleep and health does the barefoot boy enjoy?

What kind of words are the following: Ground-nut, wood-grape, and wild-flower, and is there any rule for forming them?

What figure of speech does he use in the last six verses of the second stanza?

Define the following: "ground-mole," "tortoise," "oriole," "snouted mole," "pickerel," "pied," "moil."

ORTHOGRAPHY.

[Riggs.]

1. *Give words representing all the different sounds of final* OUGH.

Ans. Bough, through, dough, tough, trough, hough.

2. *Use in words the following prefixes or modifications of them, and define each word so as to bring out the mean-*

ing of the prefix: CIS, CON, IN, JUXTA, MIS, NETHER, PER, SUB.

Ans. (*a*) Cisatlantic: *On this side* the Atlantic.
(*b*) Conjoined: Joined *together*.
(*c*) Inscribed: Written *within*.
(*d*) Juxtaposition: *Near* position.
(*e*) Misconstrued: Interpreted *wrongly*.
(*f*) Nethermost: *Below* the furtherest, the lowest.
(*g*) Perhaps: *By* chance.
(*h*) Subway: *Under* way.

3. *Give the substitutes for the long sound of* I, *and use each substitute in a word where it represents this sound.*

Ans. ie in hie; *ui* in guile; *ai* in aisle; *y* in my; *uy* in buy; *oi* in choir; *ye* in rye; *eye* in eye; *ay* or *aye* (meaning *yes*).

4. *Give accentuation, syllabication and diacritical marking of the following words: Sesame, recondite, sacrament, exemplary, enervate, gibbet, giblet, granary.*

Ans. ses′ a me, e ner′ vate,
rec′ on dite, gib′ bet,
sac′ ra ment, gib′ let,
ex′ em pla ry, gran′ a ry.

[Have not the means to represent diacritical marking.—Ed.]

5. *Discriminate between vocation and avocation; contemptuous and contemptible; respectfully, respectively, and respectably.*

Ans. (*a*) In the singular, vocation means one's ordinary trade, business or profession, while avocation means an occasional call for which a person leaves his regular employment or vocation. In the plural form, by good usage, avocation has become synonymous with vocation.
(*b*) Contemptuous means manifesting or expressing contempt or disdain. Contemptible means worthy of contempt or disdain.
(*c*) Respectfully, in a manner full of respect. Respectively, relating to each separately in order. Respectably, in a manner fitted to awaken respect.

6-10. *Spell correctly : Coochuc, sycology, movable, valour, excelent, tradegy, stragetic, gost, catif, fashon, diptheria, bronkitis, retorik, prespiration, recieve, bandana, bananna, villan, ruffin, tabood, synecure, sinosure, vittles, hippocrit, humurus.*

[See any dictionary.— Ed.]

PENMANSHIP.

[Taylor.]

1. *What training in penmanship have you had?*

[For applicant.]

2. *Do you practice slant or vertical writing? Why do you prefer it?*

Ans. I use the vertical. I prefer it because it is so easily made legible, and because it is so easily read even when written by a poor writer. It is an annoyance to even look at writing done by a pupil who writes slant, unless he is a good writer and writes a round hand nearly vertical.

3. *Define penmanship.*

Ans. Penmanship is that art which includes all work done with the pen. In the application of the term penmanship to writing there is a discrepancy as to the use of the term by the general public and special penmen. In the eyes of the public, the penmanship is bad if it is difficult to read, or good if it is easily read and presents a neat, clean appearance. With the special penman, the penmanship is good or bad as the execution of it is or is not skillfully done. This discrepancy is the bone of contention with regard to vertical writing.

4. *Discuss the different movements which may be employed in writing, naming the one you would insist upon your pupils acquiring. Give your reason for this preference.*

Ans. The movements that may possibly be employed in writing are whole-arm, muscular, finger, close (careful), free, cramped, extravagant, controlled, uncontrolled, etc. Cramped, extravagant and uncontrolled movements should always be guarded against. As to the execution of writing, I prefer that combined muscular and finger movement which naturally comes from the proper position, proper pen-holding and proper manner of movement, impelled by proper drills. Drawing and stroke-movement are terms that suggest the manner of movement. Close movement should never be that of drawing, or slow movement. It should at least be stroke-movement. Free movement should be the object of every writing exercise; but, coupled with this and never separated from it, should be correct form, which necessitates close movement while learning it accurately. With children, this learning should be confined largely to single letters and short words, and should not ordinarily be required of children younger than eight years old. Free movement is preferable to accurate form in the primary grades, but accurate form must and may be learned sooner or later without inducing a cramped movement.

5. *Write the capital letters.*

[For the applicant.]

6. *Classify the small letters as to height from standpoint of either slant or vertical writing.*

Ans. The small letters are classified as to height, as short, extended, and semi-extended letters. The short letters are said to be one space high, and others are measured by them. In vertical writing the loop letters are easily made shorter than in slant writing. In slant writing they are generally about three spaces, but in vertical writing they need not be more than two and one-half spaces. Semi-extended letters are about two spaces high; *f* is a loop letter, and extends above and below the body of the writing; *p* is a semi-extended letter, and extends above and below the body of the writing.

7. *Write a complete business letter making order for specific goods. This letter should illustrate arrangement, composition, punctuation, use of capital letters, etc.*

[For the applicant.]

8. *Examiner will grade the penmanship of the above answers at thirty per cent.*

THEORY AND PRACTICE.

ELEMENTARY EDUCATIONAL PSYCHOLOGY.

[Taylor.]

1. *Distinguish between the mind of the child and the mind of the adult.*

Ans. The child's mind is latent, undeveloped, and depends upon the senses for its knowledge. The reflective powers are weak and the reason untrained. The adult

mind draws upon its experience, is reflective, introspective, and reasoning.

2. *Compare the character of the knowledge secured by the child with that secured by the adult.*

Ans. Owing to the character of its mind the knowledge gained by the child is partial, imperfect, and defective, because it relies almost entirely upon the report of its senses. The knowledge of the adult is more abstract, general and universally true, because his analytic and reasoning powers supply him with principles and laws in addition to objects and special instances.

3. *Show how the development of the child is dependent upon physical conditions. Be specific.*

Ans. No child can be in a good condition to receive mental work and assimilate it, who is suffering from hunger, thirst, bad or cold or hot air, uncleanly body, uncomfortable clothing, or disease of any kind or character. A sound mind in a sound body is the only thing that education will develop into something high, noble, good, and useful.

4. *Name at least two classes of ideas derived through each of the special senses.*

Ans. *Sight:* Distance and color.
Hearing: Sound and distance.
Taste: Character and flavor.
Smell: Character and odor.
Touch: Size and quality.

5. *Discuss and explain the processes of association, disassociation, and attention.*

Ans. (*a*) The elements of which any experience is composed become so related in the mind by association that the recurrence of one element tends to bring back the others. Thus, at the sight of an apple, the sensation of taste returns to the mind; at the sight of water, thirst is intensified; at the sight of a fur-muff, the idea of cat is renewed in the mind; at the sound of sleigh-bells, snow and even a long ride with a spelling-contest at the close of it are brought before the mind.

(*b*) The element of an experience which possesses the most value to the child comes at once into prominence in consciousness, the others taking a subordinate place in apperception or dropping out of notice entirely by disassociation. Thus, the child learning that a certain tone or note in his voice will attract his mother's care, will use this element when she does not otherwise respond promptly.

(*c*) When the mind is concentrated upon some particular element in an experience, it is said to be giving attention. It is essential to all knowledge-getting. The isolation of the element must be complete; but there will be no meaning in it until the mind discovers correspondence between the new element and those with which it is familiar. The learner must not only look at the element, but he must be rapid and alert in fitting it into himself and his past experiences.

6. *Show how the home life and school life should articulate with each other.*

Ans. One should be the continuation and complement of the other. The habits of observation, study, self-restraint, and character-building begun in each should be continued in the other, by intelligent, active, concerted and continuous coöperation of parents and teacher.

7. *Explain motor control, and show how it is related to the every-day life of the child.*

Ans. Motor control is bringing the voluntary muscles of the body under the direction of the intellect. Until it is secured the child is awkward and unsafe. When he has acquired skill in motor control he can handle his body and its parts economically, and to his own advantage and safety. The value of it is illustrated in the control over the fingers in writing, painting, the manual arts, etc.

8. *Analyze an act of memory, and show upon what it depends.*

Ans. Memory recalls past experiences, and recognizes them when recalled. These experiences are recalled by force of suggestion or association; but when the will is brought to work, and recalls the experience with an effort after utilizing the laws of association and suggestion, memory becomes recollection. Memory acts best when the child understands a subject; which affects his personal interests and needs; of which the original impression was vivid; to which his other knowledge is definitely related; in approaching which a natural sequence is followed.

9. *Show the relation of self-activity and habit.*

Ans. The several mental activities acting and reacting upon self constitute self-activity. The process organizes self and increases its power to act. Continuing skill is developed, and then readiness and comprehension. Persisted in, tendencies and disposition are created, until at last an action by repetition is identified with self, and that action becomes habit; that is, the action, without conscious mental effort on the part of self, repeats itself automatically. The main purpose of education is to create and fix *right* habits.

10. *What are the most common physical defects among school children? How are they discovered and remedied?*

Ans. (*a*) Poor eyesight, imperfect hearing, deformed or weak arms, legs, or spine.

(*b*) By observation and testing from time to time. By regulating lights, instruction in caring for the nasal and mouth cavities and the approaches to the ears; by regulating desks, benches and seats; by telling the parents of weaknesses, and advising with them.

THEORY AND PRACTICE.

GENERAL PEDAGOGICS AND METHODS.

[Taylor.]

1. *Distinguish between* (a) *teaching and learning;* (b) *education and instruction;* (c) *imitation and understanding.*

Ans. (*a*) Teaching is the act of imparting or giving instruction concerning knowledge. Learning is the act of receiving or acquiring knowledge.

(*b*) Education is the orderly and systematic development of all the powers of an individual. Instruction is the act of imparting knowledge.

(*c*) Imitation is parrot-like; it secures the form but not the substance, the letter but not the spirit. Understanding takes both letter and spirit, and makes knowledge a part of one's self.

2. *Discuss the various limitations in the educational process.*

Ans. Limitations of nature, such as physical weakness, mental incompetency, or moral obliquity; limitations of opportunity, such as unfavorable home surroundings or neighborhood; insufficiency of material helps to secure best results, as absence of educational helps, over-crowded school, too large and too many classes, poor teacher, etc.

3. *Outline the educational and moral characteristics of the true teacher.*

Ans. Should have a thorough academic as well as professional training, supplemented by wide reading, observation and experience. Should be an even-tempered, good-natured, helpful, patient, sympathetic, Christian woman above reproach.

4. *Define knowledge, and explain its four great sources.*

Ans. (*a*) Knowledge is a clear perception of fact, truth, or duty. Locke defines it as "the perception of the truth of affirmative or negative propositions."

(*b*) Observation, reflection, reading, and association with other minds.

The first, through the senses, supplies the mind with materials of fact. The second reproduces, represents and elaborates this material. The third adds the experience and reflection of other minds as preserved in books. The fourth furnishes the experience and reflection of others in person.

5. *Explain the nature of the act of learning, and show the relation of interest to it.*

Ans. The capital activity of the mind is the elaborative process, or thought proper. In this process, which is learning, the mind reacts on the presentations made to it, and by reflection, judgment and reasoning transforms crude material into organic structure. It is evident that the most difficult thing is to bring the mind into a fit state for learning. That state must be attentive, alert and expectant. This can not be secured without enlisting the attention through exciting and holding the interest.

6. *Show what mental activities are called into exercise in three specific acts of learning you may designate.*

Ans. Perception employs the senses.

Reproduction and representation employ the reflective group.

Reasoning employs the judgment and reason.

All these must be under the control and guidance of the will.

7. *What are the effects of the teacher in relation to the act of learning?*

Ans. She stimulates the mind: by arousing the attention and interest through the best and most attractive motives; by securing and fixing good habits; by supplying the mind with new materials, and by leading it to choose the best and most effective of these materials.

8. *Explain the statement that in the act of learning the school arts should largely be an idealizing process.*

Ans. It means that the mind should be supplied by the school arts with ideals, standards by which it will be enabled to measure and determine the value and efficiency of each experience presented to it, and thus add to its own strength, develop its own powers, and add to the stock of human knowledge.

9. *Show the importance of proper organization, seating of pupils, assignment of studies, acquaintance with pupil's capacity, etc., etc., in the management of a school.*

Ans. They reduce friction, economize time and effort, cause the school or classes to move as unit masses, and, above all, establish in each pupil habits of order, discipline and obedience.

10. *Show the relation of the lower activities to the higher activities, and how the lower are involved in the higher as the pupil advances in mental power.*

Ans. The lower furnish the higher with materials upon which to begin to build, and enable them to correct their work from time to time by supplying new materials and new data as the mind proceeds from the known to the unknown, from the positive to the probable.

PHYSIOLOGY.

[Spangler.]

1. *What is a contagious disease? its cause and prevention?*

Ans. (*a*) A disease communicable by contact, by virus, or by bodily exhalations.

(*b*) It is generally believed to be caused by germs given off from the sick person, which establish themselves in the system of the person exposed, and multiplying rapidly set up in that person's system the same disease.

(*c*) Isolation, inoculation, the preservation of the system in such condition that it is not a favorable soil for the growth of the particular germs or bacilli.

2. *What is the general action of tobacco, morphine, and curare?*

Ans. They are narcotic, inducing sleep, allaying sensibility, and blunting the senses, and in large quantities producing narcotism or complete insensibility.

3. *Describe a cell. What are the differences between white and red corpuscles?*

Ans. (*a*) A minute elementary structure of which the various tissues of the body are formed. A typical cell is made up of a semi-fluid mass of protoplasm, more or less granular, generally containing in its center a nucleus, which in turn generally contains two or more nuclei, the whole surrounded by a thin membrane, the cell-wall. Some cells, notably those of the blood, are destitute of this retaining-wall.

(*b*) The red corpuscles are the smaller, circular in shape, hollowed on each face, faint yellowish red in color, and tend to gather side by side in rolls. The white are larger, have a dotted appearance, are colorless, and change their form.

4. *What are the main foodstuffs? Which is the most important, and which gives rise to the most heat?*

Ans. (*a*) Proteids, fats, carbohydrates, water, salts, oxygen (according to some authorities).

(*b*) Probably water and oxygen.

(*c*) Carbohydrates and fats.

5. *Describe the spinal cord, and what functions are ascribed to it?*

Ans. (*a*) Is a column of soft, nervous matter filling the long channel in the spinal column from which arise (each by two roots, one anterior and the other posterior) thirty-one pairs of nerves.

(*b*) It carries the volitions of the brain to the muscles and transmits sensory impulses to the brain. It also is the center in which many reflex actions originate.

6. *Where is the oxygen taken in by respiration converted into CO_2, and what becomes of the lymph of the thoracic duct?*

Ans. (*a*) In the tissues of the body, and the interchange occurs through the walls of the capillaries that supply the tissues.

(*b*) It is discharged into the left subclavian vein, which pours it into the heart.

7. *What causes coagulation of the blood?*

Ans. The formation in the liquid blood of a close network of fine fibrils called fibrin, in which the corpuscles are entangled. It is thought that when the blood leaves the blood vessels or in some way comes in contact with foreign matter, some of the white corpuscles are broken up, thus setting free a peculiar substance called fibrin ferment. It is this ferment which changes the fibrinogen into the solid fiber.

8. *Where are the salivary glands? Of what use are they? What would a section through the chest region show?*

Ans. (*a*) In front of each ear on the inside of the mouth, under the tongue, and under the lower jaw on each side.

(*b*) To moisten and lubricate the food, and to digest the starches by converting them into sugars.

(*c*) It would depend upon the manner in which it was made, whether vertical, horizontal, or from side to side. Generally, it would show the respiratory apparatus, the pulmonary circulation, the heart, the diaphragm and the gullet.

9. *Describe the inner and middle ear.*

Ans. The inner ear is an irregular chamber hollowed out of the temporal bone. Within this chamber lies a closed membranous sac, which follows all its windings. This membranous sac consists of three parts: the semicircular canals, the vestibule, and the labyrinth. In this sac is a fluid with little bodies suspended in it, and in it are distributed the ramifications of the auditory nerve. The middle ear is a cavity closed upon one side by a membrane called the tympanic membrane, and on the other, next to the inner ear, by another membrane, which separates it from the inner ear. It communicates with the outside air by means of the Eustachian tube, which opens into the mouth. From the tympanic membrane to the membrane of the inner ear stretches a bridge of little bones. The sound-waves cause the tympanic membrane to vibrate. This vibration is imparted to the bones which transmit it to the membrane of the inner ear, which membrane in turn transmits it to the fluid and the bodies suspended in it, and this fluid and the suspended bodies set up the same vibration in the branches of the auditory nerve, which in its turn carries the vibration to the auditory center of the brain, where the mind recognizes it as sound.

10. *What changes are brought about by cooking meat? What is the value of beef tea?*

Ans. (*a*) The cohesion of particles is lessened; the chemical effects of heat prepare the various elements to receive more readily the action of the digestive juices; develops the agreeable flavors which stimulate the appetite, and also the secretion of the digestive juices; the destruction of many of the germs of disease.

(*b*) It has very little nutritive value, but is generally a mild stimulant.

CONSTITUTION.

[Massey.]

1. *Name five provisions of the Articles of Confederation.*

Ans. Provided for the election of a Congress, limited its powers, and left the members' compensation to respective States electing them; created an executive department to act during the vacations of Congress, consisting of thirteen delegates, one from each state; provided for a court to try cases of disputes and differences between any two or more States; gave Congress power to declare war, and to maintain and support forces to carry on war; left with the States the power to officer the land forces raised for the defense of the United States.

2. *Explain each step in the apportionment of Representatives.*

Ans. After the decennial census, Congress determines what the total membership of the House of Representatives shall be under the new apportionment. Then, with the total population of the country as the dividend and the agreed total membership as the divisor, the basis of representation is fixed as the quotient. The total population of each State is then divided by this basis, to determine the number of Representatives to be allotted to each State respectively. A remaining fraction over half of the basis is accorded a Representative. The State then apportions its quota according to its own statutes. In Kansas the Legislature makes this apportionment.

3. *Mention four judicial powers exercised by each house separately.*

Ans. Each house has the power to judge of the elections, returns and qualifications of its own members; may compel the attendance of absent members; may punish its members for disorderly conduct; may by two-thirds vote expel a member.

4. *What is the law of Presidential succession?*

Ans. In 1886, the Presidential succession was established by law as follows: In event of both the Presidency and Vice-Presidency becoming vacant at the same time, the Presidency passes to the members of the cabinet in the order of their establishment, beginning with the Secretary of State. Should he die, or be impeached and removed, or become disabled, he is succeeded by the Secretary of the Treasury, and then, if necessary, the succession goes to the Secretary of War, the Attorney-General, the Postmaster-General, the Secretary of the Navy, the Secretary of the Interior, and presumably the Secretary of Agriculture, the head of a department created since the law was enacted.

5. *Give ten constitutional provisions for trial of criminals.*

Ans. A person charged with crime under United States law shall be presented or indicted by a grand jury; shall not be twice put in jeopardy for the same offense; shall not be compelled to testify against himself; shall be tried by a jury of the State and district wherein the crime was committed, the district to have been previously determined by law; shall be informed of the nature and cause of the accusation against him; shall be confronted with witnesses against him; shall have the assistance of counsel for his defense; shall not be required to give excessive bail; shall not have excessive fines imposed, nor be subjected to cruel and unusual punishments.

6. *Give process of admitting States to the Union.*

Ans. A constitutional convention of the Territory is called, either with or without a precedent act of the Territorial legislature. This convention frames a constitution, which is generally by its terms submitted to the people of the Territory for ratification or rejection. If ratified, it with resolutions asking for admission is presented to Congress. Congress then passes an act for admission with the constitution so adopted, with whatever conditions it may see fit to impose, as the organic law of the new State. The first legislature called under the new constitution must, in order to make the admission complete, assent by joint resolution to the terms of the act of admission.

7. *Name the Kansas courts, and tell how the highest is organized.*

Ans. (*a*) Supreme, District, Probate, Justices' courts.

(*b*) It consists of seven members chosen by the people, each for a term of six years. Four of the present court were appointed by the Governor, in January, 1901, to hold until the second Monday in January, 1903. At the general election in 1902, five justices shall be elected, one of whom shall hold his office two years, one for four years, and three for six years. At the general election of 1904 and every six years thereafter, two justices shall be elected. At the general election in 1906 and every six years thereafter, two justices shall be elected. At the general election of 1908 and every six years thereafter, three justices shall be elected. The three justices who were in office on the 2d Monday in January, 1901, hold until the expiration of the terms for which they were chosen. The seven justices may sit separately in two divisions, with full power in each division to determine the cases assigned to be heard by such division. Three justices shall constitute a quorum in each division, and the concurrence of three shall be necessary to a decision. Such cases only as may be ordered to be heard by the whole court shall be considered by all the justices, and the concurrence of four justices shall be necessary to a decision in cases so heard. The justice who is senior in continuous term of service shall be chief justice, and in case two or more have continuously served during the same period, the senior in years of these shall be chief justice, and the presiding judge of each division shall be selected from the judges assigned to that division in like manner.

8. *Name five provisions of the Clayton-Bulwer treaty.*

Ans. The United States and Great Britain stipulated for a joint guaranty of the canal to be constructed across Nicaragua, and agreed not to occupy, fortify, colonize, assume or exercise any dominion over any part of Central America.

9. *Why did the United States Senate oppose President J. Q. Adams's plan of sending delegates to the Panama conference?*

Ans. The two main reasons of opposition were:

First, the objection to an alliance, especially an armed one, with any other nation or nations.

Second, the recognition of the negro republic of Hayti, which reopened the slavery question.

10. *What action in Europe caused President Monroe to promulgate the Monroe doctrine?*

Ans. The purpose of the so-called Holy Alliance, consisting of the kings of France and Prussia and the emperors of Russia and Austria, to aid Ferdinand VII. of Spain, whom they had replaced upon his throne, to reëstablish his authority over the Spanish colonies in America, which had revolted and set up independent governments, coupled with the commercial interests of Great Britain, who for purely selfish reasons espoused the cause of the revolted colonies, caused the President of the United States to announce the Monroe doctrine.

PHYSICS.

[Spangler.]

1. *If the length of the seconds pendulum is thirty-nine inches, what is the length of a pendulum beating three times per second?*

Ans. Law: The lengths of any two pendulums are proportional to the squares of their times of vibration. Let X equal length of the required pendulum. We then have the equation $39 : X :: 1^2 : (\frac{1}{3})^2$.

$$39 \times (\tfrac{1}{3})^2 = X.$$

$X = 4.33\ \frac{1}{3}$ in., length of required pendulum.

2. *Where does a body weigh the most — at the equator, or at the poles? Why?*

Ans. (*a*) At the poles.

(*b*) Because it is nearer the center of the earth, and it has the same number of partieles drawing it to that point.

3. *Explain the principles of the lever.*

Ans. The lever depends upon two principles:

(*a*) The power multiplied by the length of the power arm equals the load multiplied by the length of the load arm. Thus, if the power arm is five times as long as the load arm, for every pound of power exerted five pounds of load will be lifted; but —

(*b*) The distance through which the power acts will be five times as great as the distance through which the load is lifted; hence the power multiplied by its velocity equals the load multiplied by its velocity, since they both will travel their respective distances in the same unit of time. Practical mechanics express this fact by the maxim, "What is gained in power is lost in time."

4. *How is power measured? What is the unit?*

Ans. (*a*) Power is the rate of doing work, and it is measured by the time that it takes it to do the work.

(*b*) The unit of power is the foot-pound-per-second, or the expenditure of energy that will raise one pound one foot high in one second of time.

5. *Distinguish between latent and sensible heat.*

Ans. Latent heat is the heat given out by a body or absorbed by it in changing its state. Thus, the latent heat of water is the heat that it parts with in changing from its liquid to its solid form, or, what is the same thing, the heat it absorbs in changing from its solid to its liquid form. Sensible heat is the heat that is measured by a thermometer. Thus, water at 32° Fahr. possesses the same sensible heat as ice at 32° Fahr., notwithstanding the fact that the water has given up many degrees of latent heat in changing to ice.

6. *On what does pitch depend?*

Ans. Pitch depends upon the rate of vibration of the sound-waves. The greater number of vibrations per second, the higher will be the pitch.

7. *What are the Frauenhofer lines?*

Ans. If light be admitted into a dark chamber through a narrow slit and received on a good flint-glass prism, it will be found not only that the colors of the spectrum are not continuous, but also that they are interrupted by numerous dark spaces. These interrupting dark spaces are called Frauenhofer's lines.

8. *What is a watt? What is the power of a current of two amperes, the difference of potential being 100 volts?*

Ans. (*a*) A watt is the practical unit of electrical activity, and it is equal to the activity exerted by one ampere passing through a circuit under the pressure of one volt.

(*b*) Wattage is power, and is equal to amperage multiplied by voltage. $2 \times 100 = 200$ watts.

BOOKKEEPING.

[Bushey.]

B. Adam began business with $4000 cash, a note of $500 given by F. Evans, and fixtures valued at $250. He owes G. Able $500 on account.

B. Adam buys merchandise, $1000, from H. Cane; pays $500 in cash, balance on account.

Pays rent in cash, $50.

Deposits $2000 in State Bank.

Pays G. Able in full with draft on State Bank.

(Draw up the above draft.)

Receives draft from F. Evans for note of $500; interest, $2.00; discount, $1.50.

Wishing to take in a partner, he takes inventory: Merchandise, $800; fixtures, $200.

1. Journalize.
2. Post.
3. Find present worth.
4. Rule a page for six-column journal.
5. Write ten abbreviations used in bookkeeping.

JOURNAL. May 1, 1901.

		Dr.	Cr.
	1		
	Cash	$4,000	
	Bills receivable	500	
	Fixtures	250	
	G. Able		$500
	B. Adam		4,250
	2		
	Mdse	1,000	
	Cash		500
	H. Cane		500
	3		
	Expense	50	
	Cash		50
	4		
	G. Able	500	
	Cash		500
	5		
	Cash	500 50	
	Discount	1 50	
	Bills receivable		500
	Interest		2 00

$500.00 Topeka, Kan., May 1, 1901.

Pay to the order of G. Able, Five Hundred Dollars, value received, and charge the same to account of

B. ADAM.

To State Bank,
No. 4. Topeka, Kan.

LEDGER.

B. Adam.

May	1	Loss.........	$299 50	May	1		$4,250 00
		Present capital.....	3,950 50				
			$4,250 00				$4,250 00

Cash.

May	1		$4,000 00	May	2		$500 00
May	5		500 50	May	3		50 00
				May	4		500 00

Bills Receivable.

May	1		$500 00	May	5		$500 00

Merchandise.

May	2		$1,000 00	May	5	*Inventory*,	$800 00
						Loss	200 00
			$1,000 00				$1,000 00

Expense.

May	3		$50 00			*Loss*	$50 00
			$50 00				$50 00

Discount.

May	5		$1 50			*Loss*	$1 50
			$1 50				$1 50

Interest.

		Gain.........	$2 00	May	5		$2 00
			$2 00				$2 00

G. Able.

May	4		$500 00	May	1		$500 00

H. Cane.

				May	2		$500 00

Fixtures.

May	1			$250 00	May	5	*Inventory,* *Loss*.......		$200 00 50 00
				$250 00					$250 00

Loss and Gain.

		Mdse .... Expense .... Discount.... Fixtures		$200 00 50 00 1 50 50 00			*Interest* ... *B. Adam* *Loss*...		$2 00 299 50
				$301 50					$301 50

Mdse. Merchandise.
Acct. or %. Account.
Amt. Amount.
B/S. Bill of Sale.
B/L. Bill of Lading.
Bgs. Bags.
Bkts. Baskets.
Bx. Box.
Exch. Exchange.
Ex. Express.

Monday and Tuesday, July 1 and 2, 1901.

ARITHMETIC.

[Nichols.]

1. *Add 5 tenths, 6 ten-thousandths, 25 thousandths; multiply the result by 5 times $1\frac{1}{2}$.*

Ans.

```
        .5                      .5 2 5 6
        .0006                        7.5
        .025                    2 6 2 8 0
sum = .5256                   3 6 7 9 2
   5×1.5=7.5                  3.9 4 2
```

The product is 3.942.

2. *Add $\frac{2}{3}$ of $\frac{3}{4}$ of $\frac{7}{8}$, $\frac{1}{4}\times\frac{2}{3}$, and $\frac{5}{6}$ divided by $\frac{4}{5}$.*

Ans.

$$\frac{2}{3}\times\frac{3}{4}\times\frac{7}{8}=\frac{7}{16}$$

$$\frac{1}{4}\times\frac{2}{3}=\frac{1}{6}$$

$$\frac{5}{6}\div\frac{4}{5}=1\frac{1}{24}$$

$\frac{7}{16}$	21
$\frac{1}{6}$	8
$1\frac{1}{24}$	2
$1\frac{31}{48}$	$\frac{31}{48}$

Sum $=1\frac{31}{48}$

3. *Divide 16 mi. 80 rds. 4 ft. by 12.*

Ans. 12 | 16 mi. 80 rd. 4 ft.

1 mi. 113 rd. 1 yd. 2 ft. 10 in.

Explanation: $\frac{1}{12}$ of 16 mi. = 1 mi., with a remainder of 4 mi.

4 mi. + 80 rd. = 1360 rd.

$\frac{1}{12}$ of 1360 rd. = 113 rd., with a remainder of 4 rd.

4 rd. = 22 yd.

$\frac{1}{12}$ of 22 yd. = 1 yd., with a remainder of 10 yd.

10 yd. + 4 ft. = 34 ft.

$\frac{1}{12}$ of 34 ft. = 2 ft., with a remainder of 10 ft.

10 ft. = 120 in.

$\frac{1}{12}$ of 120 in. = 10 in.

4. *$1200 taxes are paid on an assessment of $800,000. What is B worth, since he pays $12.75 taxes?*

Ans. Rate of taxation $=\frac{1200}{800000}=.0015$, or $1\frac{1}{2}$ mills on the dollar.
B's property $=\frac{\$12.75}{.0015}=\$8500$.

5. *A lot cost 25 per cent. less than the house on it. How much did each cost, since both cost $7000?*

Ans. 100% C = cost of house.
75% C = cost of lot.
175% C = cost of both.
∴ 175% C = $7000.
$C=\frac{\$7000}{1.75}=\$4000$.
75% C = $3000.
The house cost $4000 and the lot cost $3000.

6. *An agent sold a house and kept 4 per cent. commission, which was $8. How much did he remit to the owner?*

Ans. 4% sales = $8.
sales $=\frac{\$8}{.04}=\$200$.
Amount remitted = $200 − $8, or $192.

7. *The principal is $800, rate 6 per cent., interest $361.60. What is the time?*

Ans. $800
.06
$48 = interest for 1 yr.
No. yr. $=\frac{\$361.60}{\$48}=7\frac{8}{15}$, or 7 yr. 6 mo. 12 da.

8. *Find the difference between the true discount and the interest of $300 for 1 yr. 6 mo. at 10%.*

Ans. $300
.10
$30 = interest for 1 yr.
$45 = interest for 1 yr. 6 mo.
Present Worth $=\frac{\$300}{1.15}=\$260.87-$.
True Discount = $300 − $260.87 −, or $39.13 +.
Difference = $5.87 −.

9. *Six-per-cent. bonds are sold at 25% discount. What rate of interest will they produce on the investment?*

Ans. One share costs $75 and yields $6.
The rate of gain $=\frac{6}{75}$, or 8%.

10. *What is the length in rods of the diagonal of a section of land?*

Ans.

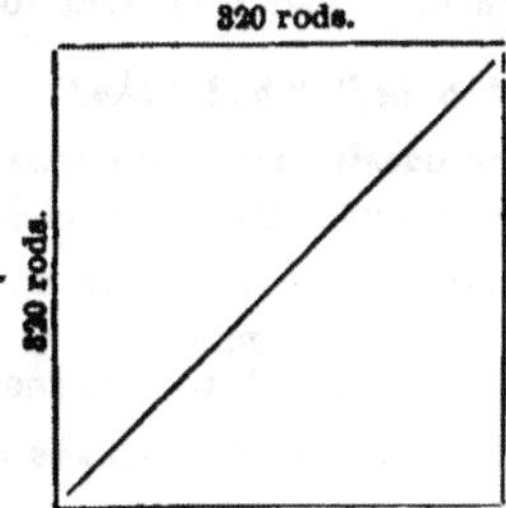

$D^2 = 320^2 + 320^2 = 204800.$
$D = \sqrt{204800}$, or 452.5+.
Diagonal = 452.5+ rds.

GRAMMAR.

[Bushey.]

"When the citizens learned that he had been sent for from Somersetshire, that he had been closeted with the king at Richmond, and (that he was *to be* the first *minister*,) they had been in transports of joy."

1. *Point out the principal clause in above sentence.*

Ans. "They had been in transports of joy."

2. *Give construction of the word* FOR *(line 1).*

Ans. Part of the verb "Had been sent for." "Had been sent for" is the grammatical predicate of the sentence "That he had been sent for from Somersetshire." It is a verb, in the third person, singular, to agree with its subject "he."

3. *Give construction of the word* MINISTER *(line 3).*

Ans. "Minister" is a part of the complement phrase "to be the first minister," which is the attribute of "he" after "was."

4. *Give construction of the clause,* THAT HE WAS TO BE THE FIRST MINISTER *(lines 2 and 3).*

Ans. One member of the compound object of "learned." The other two members of this object are the two clauses beginning with "that," in the first line, and closing with "Richmond," in the second line.

5. *Give construction of* TO BE *in said clause.*

Ans. It is the base of the complement phrase "to be the first minister," the attribute of "he" after "was."

6. *Classify the verbs as to use in above sentence.*

Ans. *Transitive* —" learned," "had been sent for," "had been closeted."

Intransitive — "was," "to be," "had been."

7. *Point out a verb in the passive voice in above sentence.*

Ans. "Had been sent for" and "had been closeted."

8. *What is the construction of* THAT *(line 2)?*

Ans. Subordinate conjunction, connecting the clause, "that he was to be the first minister" to "learned."

9. *Give a synopsis of* HAD BEEN *(line 3) in the third person singular, subjunctive.*

Ans. *Pres.*— He be. *Past* — He were. *Pres. Perf.* — He have been.

10. *Construct a sentence containing a relative pronoun with an infinitive for its antecedent.*

Ans. We were told to obey, which we cannot do in our own strength.

GEOGRAPHY.

[Nelson.]

1. (a) *Explain changes of season;* (b) *formation of rain, snow, clouds, frost;* (c) *effect of moisture upon plant and animal life.*

Ans. (*a*) Seasons are due to: the revolution of the earth in its orbit, the inclination of the earth's axis to the plane of its orbit, and the position of the sun at one focus of the orbit instead of at the center. The northern end of the axis leans towards the sun in June, when the sunshine is strongest north of the equator, and away from the sun in December, when the sun is strongest south of the equator. In the former instance summer prevails north, and winter south of the equator. In the latter, the reverse is true. The position of the sun at the focus, and the varying velocity of the earth in her orbit, give the northern hemisphere in each year five more days of vertical sunshine than is enjoyed by the southern hemisphere. Thus the sun seems to stand over the equator twice in each year, marking the beginning of spring and autumn respectively. When he seems to reach his farthest point north, our summer begins, and the farthest south, our winter commences.

(*b*) The first form assumed by the moisture of the upper air when condensed is that of cloud. If condensation continue and vapor be abundant, the small water particles will increase in size until they are too heavy to float and will fall as rain to the earth. This moisture falling through the cold upper regions of the atmosphere, if frozen in flakes forms snow. On clear, calm nights, the grass, leaves, and other objects radiate their heat rapidly and grow cold. This chills the surrounding air so that it can no longer hold the same amount of moisture as when it was warm. A portion of the moisture is condensed and stands upon the leaves, grasses, etc., in small drops of water, called *dew*. If the temperature be reduced so low that the dew freezes, *frost* is formed.

(*c*) It nourishes both. Insufficient moisture will produce disease in both. Want of it will cause death.

2. *Name and locate three important rivers in Africa, four in Europe, five in North America, and three in Asia.*

Ans. (*a*) The Nile rises in the equatorial lake region in eastern Africa, and flows north into the Mediterranean sea. The Niger rises in western Africa, near the 10th degree N. lat., flows northeast, southeast and south, and empties into the Gulf of Guinea. The Congo rises in central Africa about 6° S. lat., flows north to the equator, thence northwest to about the 2d degree N. lat., thence west and southwest, crossing the equator the second time and emptying into the Atlantic about 6° S. lat. and 14° long. west of its source.

(*b*) Volga rises west of center of Russia, flows northeast, southeast, southwest and southeast into the Caspian sea. The Danube drains Germany, Austria-Hungary, Servia, Roumania, and Bulgaria, and discharges into the Black sea. The Rhine drains Switzerland, Germany and the Netherlands, and empties into the North sea. The Po drains northern Italy and discharges into the Adriatic sea.

(*c*) Yukon rises in northwestern dominion of Canada, flows generally northwest, west and southwest through Alaska, and discharges into the Bering sea. Mackenzie rises in northwestern dominion of Canada in Great Slave lake, flows northwest into the Arctic ocean. St. Lawrence drains the Great Lakes, flows northeasterly between Canada and the United States and through southeastern Canada into the Gulf of St. Lawrence. Mississippi rises in northern United States, flows south, draining the central portion, and empties into the Gulf of Mexico. Colorado rises in western United States, flows southwest and south into the Gulf of California.

(*d*) Brahmaputra rises in south-central Asia, flows east, southeast, southwest and south into the Bay of Bengal, between Burmah and Hindustan. Yangtse rises in south-central China, flows south, southeast, north, northeast, east, northeast, into the east China sea. Hoang-Ho rises near center of China, flows north, northeast, east, south, east and northeast into the Gulf of Pe-chi-li.

3. *How would you teach form, distance, and location, in geography, to the primary class?*

Ans. By object lessons, actual measurements, etc., beginning with the school-room, and progressing to the school-yard and adjoining premises.

4. *Name and describe three important physical characteristics of* (a) *North America,* (b) *South America,* (c) *Europe, and tell what effect they have upon the civilization of the respective countries.*

Ans. (*a*) Has a great primary highland, the Rocky Mountain system, in the west; a secondary system, the Appalachian mountains, in the east; and a great central depression, the Mississippi valley and the Hudson bay and Mackenzie valleys in the interior. The presence of the Great Lakes, the low-lying Alleghanies next, the more deeply indented Atlantic seaboard, and the Mississippi connecting with the Gulf of Mexico, caused that seaboard, the lake region, and the valley to be first and more densely populated, and gave rise to the large cities to be found there.

(*b*) The lofty Andes on the west and the Guiana and Brazilian highlands on the east inclose between them the fertile valleys of the Orinoco, Amazon and La Plata rivers, all of which flow into the Atlantic. These plains and valleys make the main life of the country farming and grazing, and the outlet toward the Atlantic establishes its great States and important cities to the east of the Andes.

(*c*) Europe, with water all about her except upon the east of Russia, has numerous indentations of the seas, with fine harbors, and her main axis of elevation is from east to west. As a consequence, her great nations and cities are found mainly to the north and south of this axis, and have, or have had, the major part of the world's commerce.

5. *Describe winds, ocean currents, mountain systems, zone, continent.*

Ans. (*a*) Bodies of air in motion are called winds, and are generally caused by the unequal distribution of heat, or by the unequal distribution of vapor in the atmosphere.

(*b*) The horizontal movements of the oceanic waters cause great rivers to flow through the sea, called currents. These currents are either of warm or of cold water, while their banks and beds are water of the opposite temperature.

(*c*) Two or more mountain chains parallel or nearly parallel with one another form a mountain system.

(*d*) The earth's surface may be considered as divided into belts of temperature, vegetation, animal life, etc. These belts form zones of temperature, vegetation, fauna, etc.

(*e*) The six largest land-masses into which the earth's surface is divided by the oceans are called continents.

6. *Bound Kansas. Name and locate* (a) *principal rivers,* (b) *railroads,* (c) *educational institutions.*

Ans. (*a*) North by Nebraska, east by Missouri, south by Indian Territory and Oklahoma Territory, west by Colorado.

(*b*) The Kansas drains the northern half of the State, has for its tributaries the Smoky Hill, the Republican, and the Big Blue, and discharges into the Missouri on the east State line. The Smoky Hill receives the waters of the Saline and Solomon rivers. The Arkansas enters the State on its west boundary about one-third its breadth north of the south line of the State, and, after bending far to the north, turns south, leaving the State about one-third its length west of the east State line. The Neosho drains the southeastern part of the State.

(*c*) The Atchison, Topeka & Santa Fe runs southwesterly from Kansas City until it strikes the Arkansas river at Hutchinson, and follows that river in general until it leaves the State on west line. It has many branches by which it reaches the northeast, the central, the southeastern, the southern and southwestern portions of the State.

The Chicago, Rock Island & Pacific runs west and northwest from Kansas City, leaving the State about one-fifth its breadth south of the north line. It too has many branches north, northeast, and southwest, the latter passing through the east-central and southern sections of the State, entering the Territories south.

The Union Pacific follows up the Kansas river to Junction City, where it follows the valley of the Smoky Hill to the Colorado line.

The Missouri Pacific enters the State in Miami county, and runs almost due west, leaving the State in Greeley county. It has many important branch lines south and southwest, and a very important one in north third of State, called the Central Branch.

Other important lines are: The Missouri, Kansas & Texas; the Kansas City, Fort Scott & Gulf; the St. Louis & San Francisco, etc., etc.

(*d*) The State University, at Lawrence; the State Normal School, at Emporia; the State Agricultural College, at Manhattan; the Boys' Reform School, at Topeka; the Girls' Industrial School, at Beloit; School for the Blind, at Kansas City; School for the Deaf and Dumb, at Olathe; Institution for Feeble-Minded Youth, at Winfield; Soldiers' Orphans' Home, at Atchison.

7. *Locate the following: Japan current, Hudson bay, Rio Janeiro, Pekin, Rhone, Melbourne, Havana, Madrid, Ganges, Korea.*

Ans. (*a*) It is the north branch of the equatorial current; passes through the archipelago off the southeastern coast of Asia, turns north and east, sweeps past the Japanese Islands, passes the Aleutian Islands, receives the name of the Aleutian current, turns southeast and reënters the equatorial current.

(*b*) Large indentation of Atlantic in northeastern part of North America.

(*c*) Capital and Atlantic seaport of Brazil, situated a little north of the Tropic of Capricorn.

(*d*) Capital of China, situated near the east coast, north of the center line of the Empire. Its port is Tien-tsin, on the Gulf of Pe-chi-li.

(*e*) A river draining the eastern part of France, flowing south and discharging into the Gulf of Lion.

(*f*) Capital and seaport of Victoria, in Australia — on southern coast.

(*g*) Capital and seaport of Island of Cuba — on northern coast.

(*h*) Capital of Spain. Interior, near center of kingdom.

(*i*) A river of northeastern Hindustan, flowing southeast and discharging into the Bay of Bengal.

(*j*) A kingdom peninsula of northeastern Asia, separating the Yellow and Japan seas.

8. *Name five of the chief industries of the United States, and show their interdependence.*

Ans. (*a*) Cotton and grain growing; cattle, sheep and hog raising; woolen and cotton manufactures; milling and packing.

(*b*) The cotton-grower and sheep-raiser furnish the raw materials for the woolen and cotton factories; the grain-grower furnishes the material to the miller and stock-grower; the live-stock raiser furnishes the raw material for the packing-house products. In each instance a portion of the manufactured product returns to those who supply the raw products, and is consumed by them. The same interdependence can be shown to exist among the iron and coal mining and the steel and iron goods, and the railroads and agriculturists.

9. *Name and locate the important islands adjacent to Europe, Africa, and North America.*

Ans. (*a*) The British Isles, Faroe, Iceland, Lofoden, Balearic, Sardinia, Corsica, Sicily, the Ægean Archipelago, Crete, Rhodes, Cyprus and Malta.

(*b*) Madeira, Canary, Ascension, St. Thomas, St. Helena, Madagascar, Sokotra, Zanzibar.

(*c*) Greenland, Grinnell Land, North Devon, Parry, Melville, Banks, Prince Albert Land, Southampton, Resolution, Newfoundland, Anticosti, Prince Edward, Cape Breton, Long, Bermuda, Bahama, West Indies, Revillagigedo, Santa Barbara, Vancouver, Queen Charlotte, Prince of Wales Archipelago, Baranoff, Kadiak, Aleutian, Prybiloff, and St. Lawrence.

10. *Name the States bordering upon the Mississippi river, and give capital of each.*

Ans. Minnesota, St. Paul; Wisconsin, Madison; Iowa, Des Moines; Illinois, Springfield; Missouri, Jefferson City; Kentucky, Frankfort; Tennessee, Nashville; Arkansas, Little Rock; Mississippi, Jackson; Louisiana, Baton Rouge.

UNITED STATES HISTORY.

[Riggs.]

1. *Give an account of the settlement of Virginia.*

Ans. Three ships belonging to the Virginia Company landed the first colony on a little peninsula in the James river, about thirty miles from its mouth. There the colonists made their settlement, calling it Jamestown, in May, 1607. There were many adventurers and gentlemen of broken fortunes among their number. Their food gave out, the Indians became hostile, fever set in, and before September, 1607, half of the party had died. John Smith saved them by his resourceful energy, taking command, putting the men to work building huts, securing food from the Indians, and exploring the bays and rivers of Virginia. Then came Gates and Somers with 500 worthless men taken from the streets and jails of London, and the worse mischance of Smith's enforced return to England. Sickness and famine reduced their number to 60 in six months' time. These had gone on board ship, and sailed down the James to abandon the colony, when they met Lord Delaware with three ships filled with men and supplies, and bearing a new charter, June 8, 1610. Under these new conditions Virginia began to thrive and to exercise self-government, until July

30, 1619, at Jamestown, Virginia held the first representative Assembly ever convened by white men in America.

2. *Describe the difficulties between the Puritans and Quakers in Massachusetts.*

Ans. The Puritans persecuted the Quakers because of their peculiar religious beliefs. In July, 1656, two Quaker women who came to Boston were put in jail, their books burned, and a master of a vessel was put under bond to take them from the colony. In the same year a law was enacted prohibiting any shipmaster from bringing any Quakers to Massachusetts, upon penalty of one hundred pounds fine and taking the Quakers away again. The Quakers themselves when found were sent to a house of correction, severely whipped, and not suffered to speak with anyone. In 1658 a law of banishment was pronounced against visiting and resident Quakers, with death for a penalty in case of return after being banished. Under this law Mary Dyer and three others were hanged on Boston Common. During the persecution, which was stopped by order of the crown, fines, imprisonment, keeping in irons, boring through tongue with hot iron, whipping at a cart's-tail, and death, were inflicted.

3. *What principle was at the foundation of the establishment of Providence and Rhode Island, and how has it grown?*

Ans. (*a*) The separation of church and State; the toleration of all religious beliefs; attendance on religious service free and voluntary.

(*b*) Until religious freedom has been incorporated into the fundamental law of the National Government, of every State government, and in all territory belonging to the United States.

4. *What services did Robert Morris render to his country?*

Ans. He furnished it with the "sinews of war" during the Revolution, when disintegration and defeat seemed imminent and inevitable because of lack of money.

5. *Describe Arnold's treason.*

Ans. Arnold was put in command of West Point in July, 1780. He immediately, as he had purposed to do when seeking this command, entered into correspondence with the British General Clinton to surrender the important fortress. Clinton selected Major Andre to conduct the negotiations with Arnold. Arnold and Andre met at Stony Point and exchanged papers in September; but on Andre's return he was captured by three Americans. Arnold was informed of

Andre's apprehension, and fled to the British; served with the enemy until the war closed, and sought refuge in England. Andre was tried as a spy, found guilty, and hanged. It is believed that Arnold's main reason for his treachery was a reprimand that Washington had administered to him on account of his abuse of the government of Philadelphia with which Arnold had been intrusted.

6. *How did the invention of the cotton-gin affect the cotton industry?*

Ans. It multiplied it manifold, and made cotton the chief staple and source of wealth of the South, and building up the great cotton manufactories of the North.

7. *Give an account of Perry's victory.*

Ans. During the war of 1812, in 1813, Oliver Hazard Perry with nine small ships which his crews had built out of green timber, sought out the British fleet in Lake Erie. In the fight that followed he was compelled to abandon the flag-ship *Lawrence*, and, with his flag on his arm, row in a small boat amidst a storm of bullets to the *Niagara*. With this ship he broke the British line and captured every vessel. His dispatch to General Harrison is famous: "We have met the enemy and he is ours — two ships, two brigs, one schooner, and one sloop." The victory gave command of Lake Erie, and enabled Perry to transport Harrison's soldiers into Canada, where he defeated the British and Indians at the battle of the Thames.

8. *What was the "underground railroad"?*

Ans. It was an organization that existed during the slavery troubles of the 50's. It had for its object the aiding of slaves, escaping from their masters, to get across the Free States into Canada.

9. *Describe the legislative war of 1893 in Kansas.*

Ans. When the legislature met, Jan. 10th, 1893, it was discovered that 65 Republicans, 58 Populists and 2 Democrats held certificates of membership in the House of Representatives. The Populists had filed contests against ten of the Republicans, and omitted the names of these ten from the membership list. Sixty-four Republicans were present, and they organized by choosing George L. Douglass as Speaker. The 58 Populists organized an opposition House, with J. M. Dunsmore as Speaker. On January 12th the Republicans were reinforced by the two Democrats and Joseph Rosenthal, a Democrat, who took the place of the missing Republican, A. W. Stubbs, who refused to serve, as all parties conceded that Rosenthal had been elected to the seat for which the certificate had been granted to Stubbs. From January 10th to February 15th, 1893, both bodies continued to hold daily sessions in the Hall of Representatives. On the last-named date, the Republicans found the doors locked and the approaches thereto guarded by armed men, who were acting in the name of L. D. Lewelling, Governor of State, who, with the Senate, had recognized the Dunsmore House as the legal body. The Douglass House broke down the doors and took possession of the hall. The Governor demanded that they vacate. They refused. The Governor called out the State militia and besieged the Hall of Representatives, which was defended by about 600 sergeants-at-arms of the Douglass House. The Brigadier-General commanding the State militia, J. W. F. Hughes, refused to obey the Governor's order to expel them from the hall, and the sheriff of Shawnee county also refused the request of the Governor to interfere.

After about three days of this strained condition, a compromise was effected, by which the Douglass House was left in possession of the hall and the Dunsmore House was given a room in another part of the State House in which to meet. This status was to be and was maintained until the Supreme Court passed upon the test case of L. C. Gunn arrested by a sergeant-at-arms of the Douglass House because he had refused to obey a subpœna issued by Speaker Douglass. February 25th, the Supreme Court refused Gunn a writ of habeas corpus, and declared the Douglass House to be the *de jure* and *de facto* House of Representatives. February 28th, the members of the Dunsmore House, bearing the American flag, entered the hall and took their seats as members of the House recognized by the Supreme Court. Thus ended the war.

10. *Discuss the present relations between the United States and the Philippines.*

Ans. The Philippines are United States territory procured by cession based on purchase from Spain, and as such territory they are under the management and control of Congress.

READING.

[Massey.]

1. *Define emphasis. Give four rules for emphasis.*

Ans. (*a*) A particular stress or force of utterance of the voice given to some particular words or phrase whose significance the speaker intends to impress specially upon his audience.

(*b*) Emphasize an antithesis, either expressed or understood.

Emphasize words which express strong emotion and those in which "peculiar eminence of the thought is solely considered."

Emphasis may be used to supply an ellipsis and to suggest other words whose meaning is implied as belonging to the sense of the word emphasized.

Emphasis is frequently used to mark syntactical relations that are somewhat obscured by intervening words or phrases.

2. *Define oratorical pauses. When should they coincide with grammatical pauses?*

Ans. (*a*) Pauses made by the speaker to secure a better understanding from his audience, or to arouse their emotions and influence their convictions.

(*b*) Whenever the grammatical pauses are so placed that the speaker may by a pause in his speech at that point appeal to the understanding, imagination, reason, or sensibility of his hearers with effect.

3. *If a pupil hesitates in the pronunciation of words, what is the trouble and what are the remedies?*

Ans. He is unfamiliar with the word, or does not know how to syllabify it, or is not skilled in joining syllables in sound, or has imperfect enunciation. Practice and study will cure the defect.

4. *Name, define and illustrate each of the different inflections.*

Ans. (*a*) Grave, falling inflection on a syllable.

(*b*) Circumflex, a wave of the voice embracing a rise and a fall, or a fall and a rise of inflection on the same syllable.

(*c*) Acute, rising inflection on a syllable.

5. *Write a brief sketch of the life of any two of the following: Longfellow, Lowell, Irving, Whittier, Ruskin, Holland.*

Ans. Henry Wadsworth Longfellow was born in Portland, Maine, February 27, 1807. From both father and mother he received all the virtues of sturdy patriotism and refined intelligence which mark the old New England families. He was well educated, was graduated from Bowdoin College in 1825, and at 19 was made professor of literature and modern languages at his Alma Mater. He spent three years preparing for his professorship in visiting Europe and mastering the French, Italian, Spanish and German tongues. He began his duties at Bowdoin in 1829, and remained five years. In 1831 he was married, and in 1834 he was made professor of modern languages and literature of Harvard College, with permission to travel for a year or more. He went to Europe with his wife, who died at Rotterdam in November, 1835. Longfellow wrote in her memory the immortal "Footsteps of Angels." He began lecturing at Harvard in 1836, and continued in that work until he resigned in 1854. In 1843 he married Miss Appleton, who was burned to death in 1861. He never recovered from this tragedy, although he afterwards did some of his best work and received his greatest honors. He was made a LLD. by Harvard and a D. C. L. by Oxford, England. He died March 24, 1881, the most beloved of all America's men of letters. He was not only a great scholar and a very great poet, but he was the best poet children have ever had. He wrote Excelsior, Building of the Ship, Evangeline, Song of Hiawatha, Psalm of Life, Village Blacksmith, The Courtship of Miles Standish, and many other poems just as excellent as these. He also wrote much prose, among which appear Hyperion and Outre Mer.

John Greenleaf Whittier was a Quaker, who was born near Haverhill, Massachusetts, in 1809, and died at Hampton Falls, N. H., September 7, 1892. His was a beautiful life of love and sacrifice for others. He was the poet of freedom, and used his gifts to exterminate slavery in America. He had but one standard, that of Right. His literary style he created, his methods he formulated as he went along. He lacked education, but his "Snow Bound" is one of America's masterpieces. Of the same character are Hazel Blossoms and Tent on the Beach. But it is by his poems on slavery that Whittier has done the greatest good for man. The titles of these are numerous, but they are well represented by Expostulation, Hunters of Men, Texas, To Faneuil Hall, and The Crisis. The Kansas pioneers sang his Kansas Emigrants when they started upon their journey and while they were making this a free State. The poems of the Civil War are few, and mainly full of anxious sadness. He was a Quaker, and his religion forbade war; hence the sad note in Thy Will be Done, The Battle Autumn of 1862, and The Watchers. He wrote one poem during this period that is romantic and a favorite with all children, Barbara Frietchie. But his triumph came December 18, 1865, when slavery was abolished by constitutional amendment. Sitting in Amesbury, he heard the bells ringing that announced the glad tidings, and as they rang he sang the beautiful pæan Laus Deo. Time and space are denied us to speak of Ichabod, The Lost Occasion, My Triumph, The Eternal Goodness, Our Master, and the charming story of The School-House by the Road.

6 to 10. *Write ten suitable class questions on Longfellow's poem "Excelsior."*

Ans. What is the meaning of the title?

Did Longfellow have any special lesson he wished to teach by this poem?

Tell what that lesson is.

What does the maiden typify?

Of what is the "old man" a symbol?

How do the peasant and the old man differ?

Who were the "pious monks of St. Bernard"?

What is a "falchion" and a "clarion," and what figure of speech is expressed by both?

What is the difference between a glacier and an avalanche?

Whose voice is it that "falls like a falling star"?

ORTHOGRAPHY.

[Riggs.]

1. *Define* VOWEL, CONSONANT, TONIC, SUBTONIC, ATONIC, TRIAGRAPH, COGNATE.

Ans. (*a*) An open vocal sound modified by resonance in the oral passage.

(*b*) An articulate sound which in enunciation is generally combined and sounded with a vowel sound.

(*c*) A speech sound made with tone unmixed and undimmed by obstruction.

(*d*) A speech element consisting of vocal sound, dimmed or otherwise, modified by obstruction in the oral or nasal passage, and in some cases with a mixture of breath sound.

(*e*) An element of speech, devoid of vocality, produced by the breath alone.

(*f*) Three letters united in pronunciation so as to have but one sound or to form but one syllable.

(*g*) Two or more letters allied in origin or nature are said to be cognate.

2. *Give rules for spelling the present participle of such words as* DROP, RIDE, KILL, DIE, *and* EAT.

Ans. Dropping.— Monosyllables ending in a consonant preceded by a single vowel double the final consonant on receiving a termination beginning with a vowel.

Riding.— In derivatives formed from words ending with silent *e* the *e* is generally dropped when the termination begins with a vowel.

Killing.— Derivatives formed from words ending in a double consonant by adding one or more syllables, generally retain both consonants.

Dying.— Derivatives formed from words ending in *ie* by adding the termination *ing*, commonly drop the *e* and change the *i* to *y* to prevent two *i's* from coming together.

Eating.—When a diphthong or a diagraph representing a vowel sound precedes the final consonant of a word the final consonant is not doubled on receiving a termination beginning with a vowel.

3. *Give the substitutes for the long sound of* E, *and use each substitute in a word where it represents this sound.*

Ans. *ee* in feet; *ea* in eat; *ei* in deceive; *ie* in relieve; *eo* in people; *ey* in key; *ae* in Cæsar; *i* in machine; *uay* in quay; *oe* in Phœnix; *ue* in Portuguese, etc.

4. *What are the meanings of the word* FAST?

Ans. Abstinence from food; a time set apart to abstain from food; the act of observing the time so set apart; not loose; stable; faithful; durable; deep or sound; moving rapidly; swift; wild, dissipated or dissolute; firmly; rapidly; extravagantly or wildly; that which fastens or holds.

5. *Give rules for the hard and soft sounds of* C *and* G. *Explain the sound of the second* G *in* MORTGAGOR.

Ans. (*a*) Soft *c* has a sibilant sound of three varieties: (*a*) Like *s* sharp before *e*, *i* or *y*, as cede, civil, cypress; (*b*) Like *z* in a few words before *e*, as the second *c* in sacrifice, and in discern and suffice; (*c*) When *ce* or *ci* is followed by another vowel in the same syllable, the *sh* sound is taken by either by the *c* alone, as in oceanic and viciosity, or by the *ce* and the *ci* together, as in ocean and vicious.

(*b*) Hard *c* is the sound of *k*, and is taken before *a*, *o*, or *u*, or before a consonant, and at the end of a syllable if not followed by *i* or *e*, as cave, cold, custom, act, arc, and before *e* in sceptic and before *i* in scirrous and some others.

(*c*) Soft *g* with sound of *j* is taken usually before *e*, *i*, or *y*, as in gem, gin, stingy, and before *a* in gaol.

(*d*) Hard *g* is used before *a*, *o*, *u*, *l*, *r*, *s*, in the same syllable; sometimes before *e*, *i*, or *y*; at the end of a word and in derivatives from such a word; usually hard at the end of a syllable, as gay, go, gun, glad, dog, dogged, laggard.

(*e*) In the word mortgage the final *e* softens the preceding *g*; see rule above. Some authorities retain this *e* in forming *mortgagor*, while others omit it; but all soften the *g*, by analogy, in pronunciation.

6-10. *Spell correctly: Devellop, suthe (verb), nell, gleeb, jokand, extacy, grandure, primevil, sackrifise, privelige, hauthorne, beleve, perseve, siv, seen (a net), maskerade, rythm, conubiol, posess, selestial, terestial, mischevious, phamplet, indispensible, inaugerate.*

[See any dictionary.—ED.]

PENMANSHIP.

[Taylor.]

1. *What training in penmanship have you had?*

[For the applicant.]

2. *Argue in favor of slant or vertical writing, as you may have preference.*

Ans. I prefer vertical writing because under all circumstances it is much more easily read, and the test it has undergone proves that it can be learned easier and when once acquired it can be written about as easily and more rapidly than the slant can be written. Vertical writing is the true basis for a round style of writing, which may slant a little, right or left, from the vertical, when the writer has been forced to his individual liking in rapid business work.

I prefer the vertical because in writing it the lines do not conflict, and because the forms may be full and round, and hence it may be written with more confidence, which in itself begets ease and rapidity of execution.

3. *Describe briefly but clearly a correct position at desk for writing; include position of body, arm, hand, paper, and pen.*

Ans. Body nearly erect, leaning slightly forward from the hips, feet squarely set on the floor directly in front. Body should front the desk or table where it is possible, so that the arms may rest on the desk alike, and thus keep the body straight so that there may not be a tendency for either shoulder to droop. The hand should be in the most natural position, in keeping with the position of the body and paper.

The paper should be straight in front for learning to write the vertical; but if it be the desire of the writer to use the muscular movement, he must place the paper at an angle of twenty-five or thirty degrees with the edge of the desk, next to the writer. This may be taken up after the form has been well learned by the use of the vertical position of the paper.

The pen should be held in the thumb and first two fingers, with the thumb farther up than the fingers on the holder. The nibs of the pen should be kept squarely on the paper.

4. *Outline your method of teaching penmanship.*

Ans. My beginners in the primary grades learn enough of writing for immediate use in learning other branches, especially reading and spelling. In this I assist them to learn to write words as soon as possible, in a manner not to induce any seriously bad habits. My pupils in the second or third year are expected to begin to learn the accurate formation of the letters and the easy and rapid execution of them, and to apply them in the writing of words, sentences, and pages. This work is learned individually, each pupil mastering in a high degree each exercise as it comes in the course, and passing to the next exercise only when I have approved his work on the exercise in hand.

I am careful that the correct position of body, hand and pen be observed, and that the writing be executed no slower than would be indicated by brisk counting for the execution of the strokes. I drill the pupils occasionally in unison, by counting for them so they may understand what is expected of them individually.

5. *Classify the small letters as to height, from standpoint of either slant or vertical writing.*

Ans. There are three classes as to height: short, long, and medium. The short letters are the basis of measurement, and hence are said to be one space high; *r* and *s* are one and one-fourth spaces high. The short letters are *o, n, e, u, m, a, r, x, s, w, v, o.* The long letters are loop letters, and their maximum length above the base line is 2½ spaces, and below the base line is two spaces. They are *l, h, j, y, g, b, k, f, z, q.* The medium letters are two spaces above the base line and not more than one space below the base line. They are *t, p,* and *d.*

6. *Write all the capital letters.*

[For the applicant.]

7. *Write a complete lette making application for a position as a teacher. In this letter penmanship, arrangement, diction, punctuation and use of capital letters will be considered.*

[For the applicant.]

8. *Examiners will grade the penmanship of the above answers at 40 per cent.*

THEORY AND PRACTICE.

GENERAL PEDAGOGICS AND METHODS.

[Taylor.]

1. *Make a brief outline of mental states and activities.*

Ans. GENERAL: Consciousness, apperception, and attention.

SPECIAL: *Perceptive.*— Sight, hearing, taste, smell, and touch.

Reflective.— Memory, fancy imagination, conception, judgment, reason.

Feelings.— Animal, impulses, instincts, sensibilities.

Control.— Desires, the will.

2. *Distinguish clearly between* (a) *teaching and learning,* (b) *education and instruction,* (c) *imitation and understanding.*

Ans. (*a*) Teaching is imparting knowledge, both for its acquisition and the development of the learner's mind. Learning is receiving knowledge, and acquiring control and use of the intellectual faculties.

(*b*) Education has in view not only the acquiring knowledge, but the orderly and masterly development of all the powers of the intellect, sensibilities and will. Instruction deals with the acquiring of knowledge.

(*c*) Imitation is doing the work or performing the act done by another without knowing the principles involved or knowing the reason, scope, result, or relation of the thing done. Understanding is the knowledge of the nature, reason, scope, result and relation of the thing done or learned to other things done or learned.

3. *Show the difference between the empirical and the scientific teacher.*

Ans. The former teaches by rule, without knowing or studying the individual minds with which she is dealing. The latter instructs each individual according to the laws of intellectual development, carefully discriminating in adapting the methods and character of instruction to the idiosyncrasies of that individual.

4. *How should books be utilized in nature study?*

Ans. To supply the pupil with the mode and power of expression of others, and also give the benefit of their observation and experience after he has observed for himself; to supplement, correct, and enlarge his own work; to create a spirit of inquiry, a love for nature, and a facility, accuracy and beauty in expression.

5. *What elements enter into the act of learning and what are the essentials in the knowledge gained?*

Ans. (*a*) Interest, attention, consciousness, apperception, habit, active special faculties.

(*b*) Definitiveness, clearness, relation to other knowledge complete, usefulness or adaptibility, must have become a part of *self*.

6. *What is the relation of the teacher to the act of learning?*

Ans. That of a sympathetic guide, leader, assistant, who strives to procure favorable conditions that will enlist attention, secure interest, develop consciousness and perception, employ habit and the special faculties of the intellect; but whose duty stops here, and does not make her attempt to do the learning for the pupil.

7. *Explain the difference between the mechanical and the idealizing process of teaching the school arts.*

Ans. The mechanical is teaching the hand skill. The idealizing secures skill, but, going farther, creates a standard of beauty and usefulness in the learner's mind to which the skill is but a minister.

8. *Outline the objects of school government, and name the essentials to their attainment.*

Ans. To secure the greatest good to the greatest number in systematizing and economizing effort; to establish the idea of subordination of one's rights and privileges to the good and demands of society; to inculcate love of order in the individual pupil; to establish habits of obedience and self-control and respect for law and authority.

9. *Distinguish between positive and negative methods of instruction and show the value of incentives over restrictives.*

Ans. (*a*) In the former every good incentive to knowledge-getting and development is resorted to. Its purpose is patent and manifest. In the latter, only limitations as to action and recitation are laid down. The instruction comes from the preparation and lesson-reciting.

(*b*) Under incentives the self has a goal to reach, and every faculty is alert and tense. Under restrictions there is no goal, and effort and time are consumed in complying with the limitations, thus sacrificing the free play and healthful development of the intellect to the "Gradgrind" of "thou shalt nots" only.

10. *Show the necessity of the correlation of the work in the various grades with reference to that which precedes and follows.*

Ans. If this is not done the principle of proceeding from the known to the unknown will be violated, the orderly development of the mind will be arrested, thorough understanding will be denied the learner, and time and energy will be dissipated, never to be recovered, at his expense.

THEORY AND PRACTICE.

ELEMENTARY EDUCATIONAL PSYCHOLOGY.

[Taylor.]

1. *What is the sphere of didactics?*

Ans. Knowledge-getting and knowledge-imparting. Teaching and learning.

2. *What knowledge of mind should every teacher possess?*

Ans. Its laws and faculties; principles and laws of development; its limitations by heredity, environment and association, and the personal equation of each individual mind.

3. *Outline and differentiate the mental characteristics of the child and the adult.*

Ans. The child has his perceptive powers better developed than either the reflective powers, the sensibilities, or the will. He depends upon his senses. He is an imitator, and does not originate. He acts by rote or example, and not by reason. His imagination is active, but not under his control. The adult acts by the process of reasoning. He relies more upon his experience, and not so readily upon his senses. His perceptive powers and his sensibilities are subjected to his will. His imagination, being regulated and controlled, makes him creative and original.

4. *Outline the ideas which the child receives from each of the senses.*

Ans. Sight: Space (to a certain extent), distance, direction, color, light, shade, shape, form, etc.
Hearing: All the qualities of sound, pitch, timbre, etc., distance, direction, etc.
Taste: Flavor, quality.
Smell: Odor, quality.
Touch: Hardness, softness, smoothness, shape, form, temperature, etc.

5. *What ideas are originally obtained through touch and afterwards symbolized by sight?*

Ans. Hardness, softness, smoothness, shape, form — about all the ideas originally gained by touch.

6. *Explain how defects in sight or hearing may affect the*

child's power to gain knowledge, and show how they may be overcome.

Ans. (*a*) Such defective organs report to him imperfect and hence untrue knowledge, or perception of the external world. This imperfect knowledge forms part and parcel of all his reflection and imagination, and consequently results in his forming incorrect ideas and ideals.

(*b*) By correcting the defect as far as possible, by so arranging the environments that the error is reduced to the minimum; by paying careful and constant attention to the afflicted one in order to ascertain and correct imperfect impressions.

7. *What are the various kinds of relations, and how do they enter into the formation of mental images and knowledge in general?*

Ans. They are the connections which the mind establishes between objects of the external world, between the products of its own creation, and between objects and products. By these relations the mind sees the whole in the part, the cause in the effect, the class in the individual, and thus makes distinct and clear its images and systematizes and makes of value the materials of knowledge which it obtains by perception and reflection.

8. *What is the office of language in the knowledge-getting process?*

Ans. It is the symbolizing or expressing of the ideas by which one mind communicates with another.

9. *Show the relation of will to the emotions.*

Ans. Out of the conflict of the emotions the will idealizes, or sets up for a standard, an end to be attained, chooses the emotion or emotions to which the mind shall conform or be subject. Having made this choice, the will then proceeds to realize it. It is slow and laborious, requiring time and practice; but at last habit becomes fixed, and the emotion becomes a predominant one in the will's choice.

10. *Discuss the relations of the social, moral and esthetic instincts.*

Ans. The impulse to fellowship is the social instinct, and out of it grows the moral idea. The social recognizes the relations of individuals to one another; the moral recognizes its obligation to realize those relations, and out of both springs the esthetic instinct, which would realize those relations in forms of beauty and ideals of loveliness. These three classes of instincts are always present with the child, in play and in work, and every pleasure and every task should be so ordered that each of these shall be drawn upon and strengthened to the development of the soul.

PHYSIOLOGY.

[Spangler.]

1. *What are the anatomy and function of the cochlea?*

Ans. (*a*) It is the spiral, bony tube of the inner ear, which is coiled round a central tapering pillar of bone. Into this tube projects from the central pillar a thin shelf of bone partly dividing the tube into two parts. From the bony shelf two membranes reach to the opposite wall of the cochlea and divide the cavity into three spiral tubes. One of these tubes, the vestibular passage, connects with the vestibule. A second, the tympanic passage, connects with the membrane of the sound window. The third, the membranous cochlea, is closed at its apex, but opens near its base into the saccule. This canal contains the most delicate part of the ear, the organ of Corti. This organ is composed of pillar-like cells attached by an extended base to one of the membranes of the cochlea and ending in a swelling called a head. These pillar-like cells are called the rods of Corti. These rods are arranged in pairs, of which there are from 3,000 to 5,000, separated at their bases but leaning together above to form an arched roof. Toward the apex of the cochlea the rods increase in length, but are more widely separated at the base, making the tunnel lower and wider. Against the rods lean other cells, which end in long hair-like processes. One division of the auditory nerve passes up through a channel in the bony axis of the cochlea, giving forth fibers on its way to the bony shelf already described. These pass through and come into relation with the spinal ganglion and reach the organ of Corti.

(*b*) The cochlea alone is regarded as concerned with hearing. By the vibrations of the fluid and membrane the nerve endings in the organ of Corti are acted upon in such a way as to give rise to auditory impulses, resulting in perception of sound quality — musical notes, harmony, etc.

2. *What is the pulse, its rate, and how can it be changed?*

Ans. (*a*) The impulse from the heart's contraction felt in the arteries of the wrists, ankles, temples and other parts of the body.

(*b*) In a child, from 80 to 100 beats per minute; in adults, from 60 to 70.

(c) By age, by disease, by drugs (by narcotics and by stimulants), by exercise, by change of position, by sudden and strong changes in emotion.

3. *Describe the eye, and state the mechanism of accommodation for near objects.*

Ans. (a) The eyeball contains the most important organs of sight. It presents three coats and three humors. The three coats are: the *sclerotic*, the dense white membrane covering the ball. It is opaque, except a transparent portion in front called the *cornea*. The second coat, a colored layer, called the choroid, lying in close contact with and just inside the sclerotic, except behind the cornea, where the iris, a movable muscular curtain lined with dark pigment, is substituted for it. The hole through the center of the iris is the pupil. The third coat is a nervous membrane, called the retina, spreading out over the choroid and lining the back part of the eyeball.

The three humors are: (a) The vitreous, filling the main cavity of the ball; the crystalline lens, a transparent, lens-shaped body, inclosed in a transparent capsule, placed just behind the iris; the aqueous humor, a watery fluid, occupying the space between the crystalline lens and the cornea.

(b) The border of the lens is surrounded by a muscular ring, which by its contraction and relaxation makes the lens thicker or thinner according to the nearness or remoteness of an object to be viewed.

4. *Name the largest veins and arteries in the body, and state where they empty and arise.*

Ans. Veins.— Pulmonary: arise in each of the lungs, and discharge into the left auricle. Superior vena cava: arises in the head and upper portion of the body, and discharges into the right auricle. Inferior vena cava: arises in the lower portion of the body, and discharges into the right auricle. These veins bring to the heart the blood from all parts of the body except that from the heart itself, which is carried by the coronary vein to the inferior vena cava.

Arteries.— The great pulmonary: arises in the right ventricle and distributes the blood to the lungs. The aorta: arises in the left ventricle, and branching sends the blood to the head, upper extremities, trunk, and lower extremities.

5. *What is the difference between serum and plasma and lymph?*

Ans. The plasma is the nearly colorless fluid in which the corpuscles of the blood float.

The serum is a yellow fluid which separates and oozes from coagulated blood which has been standing for about an hour.

The lymph is a species of plasma which has passed from the blood through the walls of the capillaries into the spaces between those walls and the substance of the tissues around. It nourishes the tissue elements. It contains more water and less solid matter than does the plasma of the blood.

6. *Where is the thoracic duct, the olecranon, astragalus, atlas, and axis?*

Ans. (*a*) It runs along the spinal column upward in the abdomen and thorax, and empties into the angle of junction of the large jugular vein in the neck with the left subclavian vein.

(*b*) The large process of the ulna which projects behind the humerus and forms the bony prominence of the elbow.

(*c*) The bone of the tarsus which articulates with the tibia at the ankle; the ankle-bone.

(*d*) The first cervical vertebra, which supports the skull, being articulated by two shallow hollows with corresponding projections on the occipital bone above.

(*e*) The second cervical vertebra, articulating with the atlas above by a thick bony peg, the odontoid process, which projects into the neural ring of the atlas. Around the odontoid process the atlas rotates, carrying the head with it from side to side.

7. *What is the effect of coffee on the heart's action, respiration, and will? Tea? Alcohol? Tobacco?*

Ans. (*a*) Stimulates and then produces irregularity; quickens without supplying any food to the lung tissues; at last engenders an appetite to which the will is to an extent subordinated.

(*b*) Has same effect as coffee, in not so marked a degree.

(*c*) Increases the force and frequency of beats; takes oxygen from the cells of the heart; causes particles of the muscle-cells to become fat (fatty degeneration); hinders harmonious action of the heart nerves; at last causes the heart to beat weakly and irregularly, so that palpitation occurs on the slightest exertion. Causes thickening and distension of the capillaries and of the walls of the air-sacs, so that oxygen cannot pass through them readily. Creates an appetite that enervates, degrades and destroys the will.

(*d*) Poisons the heart muscle, causing the heart to beat with less strength; used in large quantities it has same effect upon heart nerves that alcohol has. Irritates the throat and the bronchi, producing inflammation and ulcers, keeps pure air from the lungs, and its active principle, nicotine, frequently causes disorders of the respiration which result fatally.

8. *What is the function of the pancreas, spleen, kidney?*

Ans. (*a*) Secretes digestive juice to be used in intestinal digestion.

(*b*) It is not known; but the spleen is thought to be one of the seats where red blood cells are formed.

(*c*) The kidneys perform the main work of excretion.

9. *What are the main differences between the small and large intestine?*

Ans. The small have about one-half the diameter and four times the length of the large. The small is an organ of digestion. The large is mainly a canal for excretory matter. The walls of the two are much alike, except the valvulae conniventes and villi, which are found in the small, are wanting in the large intestine.

10. *Name the sensory nerves and their distribution.*

Ans. The optic nerve, to the eyes. The auditory nerve, to the ears. The two pairs of gustatory nerves, to the tongue, palate, and pharynx. Twenty olfactory nerves, extending from the under surface of the brain, distributing themselves over the upper third of the surface of the nasal cavities.

CONSTITUTION.

[Massey.]

1. *Mention the plan advocated by at least four leaders in the Constitutional Convention.*

Ans. (*a*) The Virginia plan, drawn up and presented by James Madison, John Randolph and the Virginia delegation. Made the basis for the Constitution.

(*b*) The New Jersey plan, by all the small States, and so called from the chairman of the New Jersey delegation, Governor Patterson, who presented it. Amending articles of Confederation.

(*c*) Hamilton's plan, by Alexander Hamilton, of New York. Centralization of power in National Government.

(*d*) South Carolina plan, by Charles Pinckney, of South Carolina. Very much like the Virginia plan, but more detailed.

2. *Give all provisions regarding impeachments.*

Ans. The House of Representatives has the sole power of

impeachment. The Senate has sole power to try all impeachments; when sitting for such purpose they shall be on oath or affirmation; when President of United States is tried, the Chief Justice shall preside. No person shall be convicted except on concurrence of two-thirds of the Senators present. Judgment in case of impeachment shall not extend further than to removal from office, and disqualification to hold and enjoy any office of honor, trust or profit under the United States; but the party convicted shall nevertheless be subject to indictment, trial, judgment and punishment according to law. The President may not exercise his reprieving or pardoning power in cases of impeachment. The President, Vice-President and civil officers shall be removed from office by conviction on impeachment trial.

3. *Give ten powers of Congress.*

Ans. (*a*) To lay and collect taxes, duties, imposts and excises, to pay the debts and provide for the common defense and general welfare of the United States; but all imposts, duties and excises shall be uniform throughout the United States.

(*b*) To borrow money on the credit of the United States.

(*c*) To establish postoffices and post-roads.

(*d*) To constitute tribunals inferior to the Supreme Court.

(*e*) To declare war, grant letters of marque and reprisal, and make rules concerning captures on land and water.

(*f*) To raise and support armies.

(*g*) To provide and maintain a navy.

(*h*) To establish uniform laws of bankruptcy and naturalization.

(*i*) To coin money, regulate the value thereof, and of foreign coin, and fix the standard of weights and measures.

(*j*) To make all laws which shall be necessary and proper for carrying into execution all the powers granted, and all powers vested by the Constitution in the government of the United States, or in any department or office thereof.

4. *Explain all possible processes in the election of a President.*

Ans. (*a*) Each State shall appoint in such manner as the Legislature thereof may direct a number of electors equal to the whole number of Senators and Representatives to which the State may be entitled in Congress; but no Senator, Representative, or person holding an office of profit or trust under the United States shall be appointed an elector.

The electors shall meet in their respective States and vote by ballot for President and Vice-President, one of whom, at least, shall not be an inhabitant of the same State as themselves. The ballots for President and Vice-President shall be distinct. They shall make distinct lists showing all persons voted for as President and for Vice-President, and of the number of votes for each. They shall sign, certify and transmit, sealed, these lists to the President of the Senate at the seat of government of the United States. The President of the Senate shall in the presence of the Senate and House of Representatives open all these certified lists, and the votes shall then be counted. The person having the greatest number of votes shall be President, if such number be a majority of the whole number of electors appointed.

(*b*) If no person have such majority, then from the persons having the highest number not exceeding three on the list of those voted for as President the House of Representatives shall choose immediately by ballot the President. But, in so doing, the votes shall be taken by States, the representation from each State having but one vote; a quorum shall consist of a member or members from two-thirds of the States, and a majority of all the States shall be necessary to a choice.

(*c*) If the House of Representatives shall not choose a President whenever the right shall devolve upon it before the 4th day of March following, the Vice-President shall act as President, as in the case of the death or other constitutional disability of the President.

5. *Name all the United States courts.*

Ans. Supreme, Circuit Courts of Appeals, Circuit Courts, District Courts, Commissioners' Courts, and several limited courts created in special departments.

6. *What is the necessity of the amending clause, and what are the provisions of it?*

Ans. (*a*) To provide elasticity, so that the Constitution may fit new needs.

(*b*) Congress, whenever two-thirds of both houses shall deem it necessary, shall propose amendments, or, on the application of the Legislatures of two-thirds of the several States, shall call a convention for proposing amendments. Such proposed amendments, made in either case, shall become valid when ratified by the Legislatures of three-fourths of the States, or by conventions in three-fourths thereof, as the one or the other mode of ratification may be proposed by Congress, provided that no State, without its consent, shall be deprived of its equal suffrage in the Senate.

7. (a) *Who may vote for President in Kansas?* (b) *Who cannot vote for President?*

Ans. (*a*) All persons who may vote for a member of the

State House of Representatives. Every male person over 21 years of age, not coming under certain restricted classes.

(*b*) All males under 21 years and all males over 21 years belonging to the certain restricted classes, and all females.

8. *Give Bolivar's views regarding the consolidation of all the American republics.*

Ans. It was the great design of Bolivar's policy to unite all the republics both of South and North America into a kind of league, offensive and defensive, with a Supreme Court, which should decide such questions as are usually decided by war. Prior to this his design seems to have been to republicanize all South America by war, and then to consolidate the republics thus formed into a league, of which he should be the Protector.

9. *Give five recommendations of the Pan-American Congress.*

Ans. The Congress recommended that the republics of North and South America should adopt arbitration as a principle of American international law, for the settlement of all differences, disputes or controversies that may arise between them; a uniform system of weights and measures; uniform and liberal rules for the valuation of merchandise at custom-houses; the simplification of import and consular duties; the establishment at Washington of an international bureau of information on commercial subjects; the establishment of railways and lines of steamships among the several nations; the installment of an international bank to carry on exchange now made through London; uniformity in patent- and copyrights and trade-marks.

10. *Tell something of the attempted annexation of Santo Domingo, during the administration of General Grant.*

Ans. The agitation began in 1869. President Grant sent General Babcock and R. H. Perry to Santo Domingo, who negotiated a treaty with General Baez to annex the republic to the United States. The President urged the Senate to ratify this treaty. Senator Sumner, chairman of the Senate Committee on Foreign Affairs, opposed the ratification, and it was defeated. The President's supporters then tried to secure annexation by joint Congressional resolutions. Animated debates both in and out of both houses of Congress followed. Senator Sumner by his powerful influence defeated the resolutions, the people supported him, and the bitterest strife sprang up between the partisans of the President and Senator Sumner.

PHYSICS.

[Spangler.]

1. *Explain the parallelogram of forces. Illustrate.*

Ans. If two forces which act upon the same point are represented in intensity and direction by the adjacent sides of a parallelogram, the diagonal will represent their resultant in intensity and direction. Suppose a boat to be rowed across a stream in the direction AB at the rate of four miles an hour, at right angles to the current AC flowing at the rate of three miles an hour. Completing the parallelogram ABCD, of which AB, four miles, is one side and AC, three miles, is the adjacent side, the diagonal AD will represent the direction and the force of the resultant, or five miles an hour.

2. *What reason have we for believing the law of the conservation of matter?*

Ans. Because we cannot destroy matter. We change its form, but it will persist in some other form or forms. We burn the wood, and we simply change its form into ash, smoke, watery vapor and other gaseous substances.

3. *What is elasticity?*

Ans. Elasticity is the property by virtue of which bodies altered in form or volume by any external force resume their original shape when that force has ceased to act.

4. *Explain the action of the barometer.*

Ans. The weight of the column of mercury from the surface of the reservoir to the surface at which it stands in the tube equals the weight of the atmosphere outside, which it balances. If the atmosphere becomes denser, the mercury will rise; if the atmosphere becomes lighter, it will fall. Thus the barometer column responds immediately to changes in the atmospheric column, and thus gives warning of changes in weather.

5. *What is heat of fusion?*

Ans. The latent heat that a body has at the point of melting.

6. *What do you understand by resonance? Illustrate (sound).*

Ans. (*a*) The increased intensity produced by the commingling of direct and reflected sonorous waves.

(*b*) If a room is small, the walls not more than 35 feet from a speaker, the direct and reflected waves will strike the auditor's ear at about the same time, and the original sound will be strengthened with no diminution of clearness. In large halls the direct and reflected waves only partially coincide and the words are less distinct. The defect can be cured by furniture, dresses of audience, galleries, etc. In large rooms resonance is desirable, and is secured by arranging good reflecting surfaces of proper form behind the speaker.

7. *What is a spectrum? How obtained?*

Ans. (*a*) The colored band or image formed by dispersing a pencil of light into its constituent colors.

(*b*) By placing a refracting prism in the path of a pencil of light which has been admitted to a darkened room through a narrow aperture. If the pencil be of solar light the colors secured after being passed through the prism and received upon a screen will be seven, viz.: red, orange, yellow, green, blue, violet, indigo.

8. *What is Ohm's law? A current of one ampere flows through a lamp under a difference of potential of 50 volts; what is the resistance of the lamp?*

Ans. (*a*) The current which passes through any circuit is inversely proportional to the resistance of the circuit and directly proportional to the electro-motive force acting on that circuit.

(*b*) Ohm's law may be expressed as current-electro-motive force ÷ resistance; or, amperes = volts ÷ ohms. Then, $1 = \frac{50}{x}$. $x = 50$ ohms resistance.

BOOKKEEPING.

[Bushey.]

1. *Write six day-book entries, at least one to contain the draft principle.*
2. *Rule for special column journal, and journalize in same.*
3. *Post above entries.*
4. *Make balance-sheet.*
5. *Reopen ledger, ready to continue business.*

July 3, 1901.			
James Perry commenced business investing cash, $3000			$3000
July 5.			
Bought for cash mdse			250
July 6.			
Sold James Gray on acct. bill of mdse			320
July 7.			
Paid store rent in cash			35

July 8.			
Received cash of James Gray on account.......			15
July 10.			
Drew a draft on James Gray for $200 which I discounted at bank, receiving cash, $198....	$198		
Discount, $2....................................	2		200
Jan. 10.			
Inventory of mdse., $80.			

Mdse.	Cash.	Sundries.		July 3.		Sundries.	Cash.	Mdse.
	$3000			Cash.				
				James Perry..	40	$3000		
				July 5.				
$250				Mdse.				
				Cash..........			$250	
				July 6.				
		$320	40	James Gray.				
				Mdse.........				$320
				July 7.				
		35	40	Expense.				
				Cash..........			35	
				July 8.				
	15			Cash.				
				James Gray...	40	15		
				July 10.				
	198			Cash.				
		2		Discount.				
				James Gray ..	40	200		
$250	$3213	$357				$3215	$285	$320

James Perry.

		Present Worth....	$3113	July	3		$3000
						Gain	113
				July	10	Present Worth..	$3113

Merchandise.

July	10		$250	July	10		$320
		Gain	150			*Inventory* ...	80
			$400				$400
July	10	Inventory...	$80				

Cash.

July	10		$3213	July	10		$285

Expense.

July	7		$35			*Gain*	$35

James Gray.

July	6		$320	July	8		$15
				July	10		200

Discount.

July	10		$2			*Loss*	$2

Balance Sheet July 10.

			Loss.	Gain.	Resources.	Liabilities.
James Perry...........		$3000				
Merchandise...........	$250	320		$150	$80	
Cash..................	3213	285			2928	
Expense...............	35		$35			
James Gray............	320	215			105	
Discount..............	2		2			
	$3820	$3820	$37	$150	$3113	
Net Gain			113			
			$150	$150		
James Perry net credit.		$3000				
James Perry net gain..		113				
James Perry present capital............						$3113
					$3113	$3113

Monday and Tuesday, July 29 and 30, 1901.

ARITHMETIC.

(Nichols.)

1. *If 26 bushels of wheat make 6 barrels of flour, how many bushels will be required to make 156 barrels?*

Ans. If 26 bu. of wheat make 6 bbl. of flour, it will take $4\frac{1}{3}$ bu. to make 1 bbl. of flour. To make 156 bbl. of flour, it will take 156 times $4\frac{1}{3}$ bu., or 676 bu. of wheat.

2. *Find the interest on $684.25 for 2 yr. 6 mo. 18 da., at 5 per cent.*

Ans. The interest on $1 at 5% for 2 yr. 6 mo. 18 da. is $0.1275. The interest on $684.25 is $684\frac{1}{4}$ times $0.1275, or $87.24+.

3. *Reduce .845 mi. to lower denominations.*

Ans. 320 = No. rds. in a mile.
.845 mi. = .845 × 320 rds. = 270.4 rds.
.4 rds. = 2.2 yds.
.2 yd. = .6 ft. = 7.2 in.
∴ .845 mi. = 270 rds. 2 yds. 7.2 in.

4. *Find the least common multiple of 189, 153, and 144.*

Ans.

3	189, 153, 144
3	63, 51, 48
	21, 17, 16

L. C. M. = 3 × 3 × 21 × 17 × 16 = 51408.

5. *A man bought a rectangular field containing 3750 sq. rds., the length of which was 75 rds., at $15 per acre; what was its breadth and what did it cost?*

Ans. No. rds. in width $= \frac{3750}{75} = 50$

No. acres $= \frac{3750}{160} = 23\frac{7}{16}$

Cost $= 23\frac{7}{16} \times \$15 = \$351\ 56\frac{1}{4}$

6. *A quarter-section of land was sold for $4563, which was 8 per cent. less than cost; what was the cost per acre?*

Ans. 92% of cost = $4563

$$\text{Cost} = \frac{\$4563}{.92} = \$4959.78+$$

$$\text{Cost per acre} = \frac{\$4959.78+}{160} = \$30.99+$$

7. *If 3 men can do a piece of work in 6 days, working 10 hours a day, how long will it take 16 men to do twice the amount of work, working 9 hours a day?*

Ans.
$$\left.\begin{matrix} 16:3 \\ 9:10 \\ 1:2 \end{matrix}\right\} :: 6 \text{ days} : x$$

$$x = \frac{6 \times 3 \times 10 \times 2}{16 \times 9} = 2\tfrac{1}{2}$$

∴ It will take 2½ days.

8. *Bought stock at par and sold it at 3 per cent. premium, thereby gaining $750. How many shares of $100 each did I buy?*

Ans. 3% par = $750

$$\text{Par} = \frac{\$750}{.03} = \$25000$$

$$\text{No. sh.} = \frac{25000}{100} = 250$$

9. *Extract the cube root of 1.74088 to three decimal places.*

Ans. 1.740880 | 1.202+

	1
300	740
60	
4	
364	728
*43200	12880
4320000	12880000
7200	
4	
4327204	8654408

Rem. = .00425592

Ans., 1.202+

10. *If A puts in $4000 for 8 mo., B $6000 for 7 mo., and C*

*Annex a zero to the root and proceed as before.

$3500 for 1 yr., and they gain $2320, what is each partner's share?

Ans. A's investment = $4000 × 8 = $32000 for 1 month
B's " = $6000 × 7 = $42000 " " "
C's " = $3500 × 12 = $42000 " " "
Total " = $116000 for 1 month

A has $\frac{8}{29}$ of the investment and receives $\frac{8}{29}$ of the gain, or $640.

B has $\frac{21}{58}$ of the investment and receives $\frac{21}{58}$ of the gain, or $840.

C has $\frac{21}{58}$ of the investment and receives $\frac{21}{58}$ of the gain, or $840.

GRAMMAR.

[Bushey.]

"A more perfectly fitted and furnished character has never appeared on the theater of human action than when, reining up his war-horse beneath the majestic and venerable elm, still standing at the entrance of the old Watertown road upon Cambridge common, George Washington unsheathed his sword, and assumed the command of the gathering armies of American liberty. Those who had despaired, when they beheld their chief despaired no more."

1. *Give construction of* reining *(line 2).*

Ans. "Reining up" is the present active participle of rein up, and as an adjective element it modifies "George Washington."

2. *Give construction of* than *(line 2).*

Ans. Is a participle used after "more" to express the comparison between that portion of the sentence which precedes it and that which follows it.

3. *What does the phrase* beneath . . . elm *(lines 2 and 3) modify?*

Ans. Adverbial phrase, modifying "reining up."

4. *Give all the modifiers of* elm *(line 3).*

Ans. "Majestic," "venerable," "still . . . common."

5. *Give construction of* those *(line 6).*

Ans. Subject of the sentence, and agrees with the verb. the second "despaired," in number and person.

6. *Give construction of* more *(line 7).*

Ans. Adverb, modifying second "despaired."

7. *Give mode and tense of each of the following verbs:* has appeared *(line 1)*; unsheathed *(line 4)*; had despaired *(line 6)*.

Ans. (*a*) Indicative mode, present-perfect tense.

(*b*) Indicative mode, past tense.
(*c*) Indicative mode, past-perfect tense.

8. *Write a sentence containing an infinitive used without* to.

Ans. Let me sing.

9. *Write a sentence containing a participle used as the object of a preposition.*

Ans. We wait for his returning.

10. *Give a synopsis of the verb* have *through the third person singular of the indicative.*

Ans. Pres., He has; *Past*, He had; *Future*, He will have; *Pres. Perf.*, He has had; *Past Perf.*, He had had; *Future Perf.*, He will have had.

GEOGRAPHY.

[Nelson.]

1. *Define plateau, zenith, equator, geyser, river basin, peninsula.*

Ans. (*a*) A plain which stands high above the sea-level.
(*b*) The point of the heavens directly overhead.
(*c*) The imaginary great circle on the earth's surface everywhere equally distant from the poles, and dividing the earth's surface into two hemispheres.
(*d*) A boiling spring which sends forth at intervals jets of water, mud, etc., driven up by the expansive force of steam.
(*e*) All the land which sheds water into a single river system.
(*f*) A portion of land almost surrounded by water.

2. *Compare fully the Pacific with the Atlantic slope of North America.*

Ans. The Atlantic is a low-lying plain, situated at the foot of low mountain ranges, broken by numerous indentations and arms of the sea, with rivers which run far inland.

The Pacific plain is not so wide, even wanting in many instances; with lofty mountains rising high and abruptly, with few important harbors, and very few streams which rise far inland.

3. *Name and locate Pyrenees, Luzon, Honolulu, St. Petersburg, Chili, Stockholm, Cypress, Vancouver, Ecuador, Vera Cruz.*

Ans. (*a*) A range of mountains in the northern part of

Spain, and helping to raise a natural barrier against France.

(*b*) The largest of the Philippine Islands, lying between 11° and 14° N. Lat. and just east of the 120th meridian E. Lon. from Greenwich.

(*c*) Capital city of Hawaiian Islands, on Oahu Island, 21½° N. Lat. and 157¾° W. Long. from Greenwich.

(*d*) The capital of Russia, in northwestern part, on the Gulf of Finland.

(*e*) A State of South America lying west of the Andes, and extending from about 18° to about 52° S. Lat.

(*f*) Capital of Sweden, in eastern part, on coast of the Baltic sea.

(*g*) An island in the extreme eastern portion of the Mediterranean sea, off the coast of Turkey.

(*h*) A large island belonging to British Columbia, just off the northwestern extremity of Washington State.

(*i*) A State of South America lying across the equator, and bounded by Colombia on the north, Peru and the Pacific ocean on the south, and by Peru and the Pacific on the west.

(*j*) A division of Mexico, forming a part of the east coast bordering upon the Gulf of Mexico and the Gulf of Campeche. Also, the name of its principal city.

4. *Name six important products of Europe, and tell to what countries they are exported.*

Ans. France — Silk and wine to Great Britain and United States.

Germany — Sugar and toy goods to Great Britain and United States.

Switzerland — Silks, cottons and watches to France, Germany and the United States.

Belgium — Linen manufactures, woolen yarns, glass and glass wares to France, Germany, Great Britain, and United States.

Holland — Cinchona bark, coffee and sugar (from her colonies) to France, Germany, England, and United States.

Russia — Corn, flax, hemp, raw wool to Germany and Great Britain.

5. *Name the physical and climatical conditions of South America, and explain how they affect animal and vegetable life.*

Ans. (*a*) South America is composed of a western slope, short, and generally steep; the Andes Highland, a great mountain system with many long and high valleys between its ranges; the eastern great plains. In the valley of the Amazon these plains are forests, but in other parts mainly grass lands. They are broken on the northeast by the Guiana highland and on the southeast by the Brazilian highland.

(*b*) The north and middle parts are in the trade-wind belts, and have frequent rains. The equatorial rain-belt also shifts north and south across the northern half of the continent. The southern half reaches far into the cool belt in the path of the stormy westerly winds. The warm equatorial currents of the Atlantic moving westward under the trades, divide on the eastern point and sweep along the northeast and southeast coasts. The continent turns the cold water of the southern ocean northward along the west coast, and the winds blowing ashore are cold in the south but grow warm nearer the equator.

(*c*) In the high Andes are found stunted vegetation, the wool-bearing llama and alpaca, and the puma and condor. In the warm, moist regions the vegetation is luxuriant,— orchids, rubber trees, immense ferns, canes and grasses are abundant; animals are numerous, numbering among them armadilloes, sloths, lizards, peccaries, alligators, monkeys, tapir, jaguar, parrots, boa, and many poisonous reptiles.

In the pampas and grass plains are distributed the subtropical and temperate vegetation,— coffee, rubber, banana, etc., and the vicuna, guanaco, rhea, cattle, sheep, and horses. These cattle and sheep are not natives, having been brought from Europe.

6. (a) *Name the principal natural resources of Kansas.* (b) *Name and locate the charitable and reformatory institutions.* (c) *Name and locate five principal cities of the State.*

Ans. (*a*) Wheat, corn, oats, potatoes, hay and other crops; salt, lead, zinc, ochre, clays, gypsum, coal, natural gas, oil-wells, and building-stone; cattle, sheep, hogs, and dairy products.

(*b*) Topeka State Hospital, Topeka; Osawatomie State Hospital, Osawatomie; Boys' Industrial School, Topeka; Girls' Industrial School, Beloit; School for the Deaf, Olathe; School for the Blind, Kansas City; State School for Feeble-Minded Youth, Winfield; Soldiers' Orphans' Home, Atchison; Industrial State Reformatory, Hutchinson; possibly State Penitentiary, Lansing.

(*c*) Kansas City, eastern, in Wyandotte county, at confluence of Kansas and Missouri rivers; Topeka, eastern, in Shawnee county, on both sides of Kansas river; Wichita, southern, in Sedgwick county, on the Arkansas river; Leavenworth, northeastern, in Leavenworth county, on the Missouri river; Fort Scott, southeastern, in Bourbon county.

7. *Locate six important islands of the world, and give their commercial value.*

Ans. British Islands, in north Atlantic ocean, one of the most important exporting and importing countries of the globe.

Australia, in south Pacific and Indian oceans, the island continent, great producer and exporter of gold, sheep and cattle products.

Trinidad, off north coast of South America, great supply of asphalt.

Sumatra, off southeast Asia, in China sea and Indian ocean, spices, cotton, camphor, pepper, etc., exported.

Cuba, off soutl ıst North America, in Gulf of Mexico, Carribean sea and Atlantic ocean, tobacco, sugar, exports.

Hawaiian Islands, in mid-Pacific, sugar export, and on navigation lines to North America from Asia and Australia.

8. *Compare the Mississippi basin with the Nile basin,* (a) *as to size,* (b) *resources,* (c) *commercial advantages.*

Ans. (*a*) Mississippi: Length, 4,200 miles; basin area 1,250,000 square miles.

Nile: Length, 4,000 miles; basin area, 1,400,000 square miles.

(*b*) Mississippi: All the products of broad, fertile, t ıperate plains,—sugar, tobacco, cotton, rice, corn, wheat, oats, potatoes, fruits ranging from banana and orange to the apple and peach, plum, pear and grape; pineries, oak and hardwood forests, cane, mahogany, and subtropical woods; coal, iron, lead, zinc, gas, oil in abundance; cattle, sheep, hogs.

Nile: A narrow valley, much of it through deserts; products and fruits of subtropic and tropic clime; dates, rice, wheat, sugar cane, cotton; stone quarries; cattle and sheep.

(*c*) Mississippi: Has thousands of miles of navigable waters, leading from the sea to every part of great fertile plains, and becomes broader and deeper as it nears the sea.

Nile: Is open to large vessels only about 500 miles from the sea, and for that distance has not a single tributary. It becomes narrower and shallower as it approaches the sea.

9. *What elements of geography would you emphasize in a primary class? Why?*

Ans. Local geography, distance, direction and comparison; because the child can proceed correctly only from the known to the unknown, and he must know intimately those things with which he comes in contact before he can form any intelligent ideas concerning those which are remote.

10. *Give reasons why each of the following are important commercial centers: New York, San Francisco, New Orleans, Havana, Liverpool, Rio Janeiro.*

Ans. (*a*) Age, early settlement, fine harbor on coast fronting the great civilized nations of the Old World.

(*b*) Fine harbor, midway United States on west coast, port for Hawaii, Alaska, the Philippines, and the Pacific trade.

(*c*) Situation at mouth of Mississippi, near Gulf of Mexico, makes it great emporium for Gulf and Mississippi States.

(*d*) Havana, capital, fine harbor, largest city of Cuba.

(*e*) Principal port for the manufacturing districts of England. Receives the raw goods as imports; ships manufactured goods as exports.

(*f*) The finest harbor in the world. Is the port for the large agricultural region, which makes it the greatest coffee market on the globe.

UNITED STATES HISTORY.

[Riggs.]

1. *Sketch the life of Columbus.*

Ans. Columbus was a native of Genoa, in Italy. He began a seafaring life at 14, and became proficient in making maps and globes. About 1470 he went to Portugal, and made several voyages down the west coast of Africa. In 1473 he married a Portuguese woman, daughter of a noted navigator, who left her many valuable charts and notes. Studying these, Columbus conceived the thought of reaching India by sailing due westward. He made attempt after attempt to get monarchs, and those possessed of power and money, to assist him. At last, in 1492, under the patronage of Queen Isabella of Spain, he set sail with three caravels from the port of Palos, Spain. Sailing to the Canaries, he turned west from those islands. After a trying voyage, during which his crews mutinied, he landed on one of the Bahama Islands, October 12, 1492, and took possession of it in the name of Ferdinand and Isabella, King and Queen of Spain. He coasted Cuba, touched upon many islands, and left a colony at Haiti, returning to Spain, March 15, 1493. Afterwards he made three more voyages to the New World, discovering Jamaica, Puerto

Rico, islands of the Caribbean sea, Trinidad, sighted the South-American continent, and explored the shores of Honduras and the Isthmus of Panama, seeking for a strait leading to the Indian ocean. Of course he did not find it, and returning to Spain, poor and broken-hearted, he died May 20, 1506, ignorant of the fact that he had discovered a new world.

2. *What rightful claim, if any, has the Indian upon the National Government of to-day?*

Ans. The white men took up his lands and entered into treaties with him guaranteeing him assistance and protection under certain conditions. These treaties and guaranties the Government has confirmed and renewed, time and again.

3. *How did the cultivation of rice and indigo affect the prosperity of South Carolina?*

Ans. It made South Carolina one of the wealthiest and most influential of the colonies. Charleston became a great commercial center and port.

4. *Why was the "era of good feeling" so called?*

Ans. From 1816 to 1824 in American politics was known as the "era of good feeling," because there was but one political party, the Republican, and party feeling had of course disappeared.

5. *Describe the struggle between the Pro-Slavery and the Anti-Slavery forces for the possession of Kansas.*

Ans. In 1854, Senator Douglas introduced the Kansas-Nebraska Bill, which expressly repealed the Missouri Compromise and opened the country north of 36° 30′ to slavery, with the doctrine of popular sovereignty; that is, permitting settlers of the Territories to declare either for freedom or slavery. After a bitter contest, the bill became law, and the Free-State men from the North and Slave-State men from the South made a rush to struggle for possession. Now began a seven-years struggle for Kansas. Never were graver outrages perpetrated upon the ballot-box or the liberties and rights of men. Elections were controlled by force; non-residents denied residents the right of suffrage; legislatures were stolen; pliant tools of the slave oligarchy were sent to administer the government of the Territory; justice was corrupted; intimidation, fraud, perjury, arson and assassination ran riot. Of course it became a subject engrossing the consideration of the nation. All other questions were forgotten; it formed the theme for the Lincoln-

Douglas debates, and for notable orations in the Senate, because of one of which Senator Sumner was brutally assaulted by Senator Brooks of South Carolina; and it culminated at last in John Brown's raid, the election of President Lincoln, and the firing upon Fort Sumter about ten weeks after Kansas became a State with a free constitution.

6. *What was Lincoln's attitude regarding slavery at the beginning of his administration?*

Ans. That it should remain where it was. He would save the Union, with or without slavery; but he would save it at all hazards. He said: "I have no desire directly or indirectly to interfere with the institution of slavery in the States where it exists."

7. *Describe the Mason and Slidell incident.*

Ans. Captain Wilkes, of the United States ship San Jacinto, stopped the British mail steamer Trent in the Bermuda Channel, boarded her, and took off James M. Mason, John Slidell, and their secretaries. Mason and Slidell had been sent out as Confederate commissioners to Great Britain and France. Wilkes had no right to do this, and our Government could do nothing else than release the prisoners, place them on another English ship, and send them to England. England was unnecessarily blustering, abusive and insulting in demanding this action, which our government had never thought of refusing.

8. *Discuss the impeachment of President Johnson.*

Ans. Andrew Jackson arrogated the work of reconstructing the Southern States to himself, placed himself in defiance to the plain powers of Congress, vetoed legislation, abused Congress in popular addresses, refused to obey the Reconstruction Act and the Tenure-of-Office Act, assumed to remove a member of cabinet and practically name his successor without the consent of the Senate. For this the House of Representatives impeached him, and the Senate tried him, but failed to find him guilty by but one vote short of the necessary two-thirds.

9. *What is the ideal civil-service system?*

Ans. One in which all the clerical and merely ministerial positions are filled by men and women chosen for their special fitness, who cannot be removed save on account of incapacity for or failure to perform their duties, regardless of their politics and party affiliations.

10. *What are the main provisions of the Porto-Rican tariff act?*

Ans. The Porto-Rican tariff has been suspended. Free trade now prevails between the island and the rest of the country. It was a reduced tariff, placed temporarily upon the Porto-Rican imports to the United States to meet the extraordinary charges of establishing a settled government in Porto Rico.

READING.

[Massey.]

1. *Mention five points that you would consider in the selection of a set of readers for school use.*

Ans. Character of the selections; quantity and value of the notes and helps; the skill and judgment used in arranging selections in each book; the grading of each book with regard to the one above and below it; the size and clearness of the type; the number, character and artistic value of the illustrations; quality of the paper; kind and serviceableness of the binding.

2. *Define reading.*

Ans. The artistic, forceful and clear presentation and interpretation of the thought of another by the use of the voice, features, expression, and gesture.

3. *Name the physical qualifications of a good reader; the mental qualifications.*

Ans. (*a*) Fine presence, pleasing face and expression, graceful, easy poise and carriage of body, good lung-power, comp'ete command over well-trained vocal organs, mastery of respiratory apparatus, a pleasing, well-modulated voice of excellent timbre, quality and strength, perfect direction of muscles and of legs and arms. Superb health and great powers of endurance.

(*b*) Must have good memory, quick perceptions, lively imagination and understanding, quickness and sensitiveness of feeling, a great sense of humor as well as pathos, of the sublime as well as the ridiculous, must know and sympathize with his fellows; and all this must be under the management of a person fitted to choose, to command and to execute.

4. *What is the relation of volume to force?*

Ans. Force has reference both to the loudness of sound and intensity of utterance. Volume is the carrying capacity of the voice, and depends upon the element of force, since it is the property by which the voice sets large volumes of air in motion.

5. *Explain your method of teaching the sounds of letters to the chart class.*

Ans. By having them practice on the separate sounds both as individuals and in concert after me and from the chart. By making simple combinations of two or more sounds which they have mastered as they appear in syllables and words.

6-10. *Mention ten things in the poem, Barbara Frietchie, that will appeal to the interest of a pupil in the fourth-reader class.*

Ans. The unique personality of Barbara Frietchie herself.

The historical interest that centers about Jackson and the Shenandoah Valley.

The dash and spirit of the poem.

The colloquy that it contains.

The martial movement of its lines.

The air of adventure that surrounds it.

The sense of nearness which makes it a part of his daily living.

The description of the Rebel soldier on a march.

The contrast between the old lady and the Rebel chieftain.

The appeal to patriotism.

ORTHOGRAPHY.

[Riggs.]

1. *Give the substitutes for the long sound of* a, *and use each substitute in a word where it represents this sound.*

Ans. Ai in pain, *ay* in day, *ao* in gaol, *au* in gauge, *ea* in break, *ei* in veil, *ey* in whey, *aye* in aye (ever).

2. *Accentuate, syllabicate, and mark diacritically;* profile, orthoepy, deficit, aspirant, opponent, gherkin, precedence, hostage.

[See dictionary.]

3. *Explain the difference in meaning of the following pairs of plurals:* brothers, brethren; dice, dies; peas, pease; pennies, pence; indexes, indices.

Ans. (*a*) The former is generally the common form for pluralizing brother used in the primary sense. The latter is the solemn form, and is used in speaking of religious sects, or fraternities or their members.

(*b*) Dice is the plural form of die, a small cube used in gambling. Dies is the plural form for the die of architecture or of mechanics and machinery.

(*c*) Peas is used as the plural form of pea, both when a definite number more than one is meant and when used collectively. Pease is used in the collective sense only.

(*d*) Indexes is the English plural of index and indices is the Latin. They are generally used interchangeably; but when index is used in its technical mathematical sense, its plural form is always indices.

4. *Write the plural of each of the following words:* veto, canto, echo, memento, stratum, crisis, beau, seraph, bandit, son-in-law.

Ans. Vetoes, cantos, echoes, mementoes, strata, crises, beaux, seraphs (English form) and seraphim (Hebrew form), bandits (English form) and banditti (Italian form) was formerly used as the collective form; sons-in-law.

5. *Give a rule for the use of* ei *and* ie *in the spelling of words.*

Ans. No rule can be given. It is probably true that in a majority of instances *c, h, n, r, s,* and *w,* are followed in the same syllable by *ei,* as ceiling, receive, receipt, heinous, heir, their, heigho, heifer, height, neigh, neighbor, neither, reign, rein, reiver, reigle, reichstag, seiches, seid, seidlitz, seignior, seine, seirfish, seismic, seize, seizin, weigh, weir, weird; that *v* takes *ei* and *ie* in about an equal number of instances, as vein, veil, vie, view; that all other consonants take *ie* in a majority of cases, as bier, die, fie, fief, fierce, fiend, field, lie, lief, liege, lieu, tie, tierce, tier; that important exceptions make the foregoing suggestions of little value, as cierge, enciente, deign, feign, feint, forfeit, chief, hie, leisure, grief, retrieve, reprieve, sieve, sieur, siege, skein, and many others demonstrate.

6-10. *Spell correctly: The possessive singular and the nominative and possessive plural of* lady, boy, child, *and* man; *and the following words: silligizm, sensuus, quire (singers), leppard, amerus, epissel, parallisis, volcanose, porselin, oshun, soshul, byoo, mantanance, envelop (noun and verb).*

Ans.	*Poss. Sing.*	*Nom. Plu.*	*Poss. Plu.*
	lady's	ladies	ladies'.
	boy's	boys	boys'.
	child's	children	children's.
	man's	men	men's.

[For the spelling of the misspelled words, see any dictionary.— Ed.]

PENMANSHIP.

[Wilkinson.]

1. *What training in penmanship have you had?*

[For the applicant.]

2. *In what way is vertical writing preferable to slant?*

Ans. Vertical writing is preferable to slant because it can be written in round, full forms, which makes it much more legible. Because of this fact, and the fact that the lines do not conflict as they do in slant writing, vertical writing may be executed with a great deal more confidence, and hence, more rapidly.

3. *What are common defects in penmanship?*

Ans. Irregular and incomplete forms, and a lack of freedom of movement.

4. *Is involuntary action in writing desirable? Give your reason for your answer.*

Ans. Yes. So that the execution of the words will not occupy the mind while expressing thought on other subjects. Writing becomes involuntary action sooner or later with all who do much writing.

5. *Write the small letters, first, singly; second, in groups of four or five letters each.*

Ans. Writing for the applicant. The groups of small letters are: First group, *i, n, e, u, m, a;* second group, *l, h, j, y, g;* third group, *t, p, d;* fourth group, *r, x, c, s, w, v, o;* fifth group, *b, k, f, z, q.*

The first, second and third groups comprise all the letters of simple strokes. The fourth and fifth groups comprise all letters not of simple strokes. It will be observed that the fourth group may be considered a cognate of the first group, and the fifth group a cognate of the second group.

The order of groups corresponds with the ease with which the letters are learned and written.

6. *Write the capital letters.*

[For the applicant.]

7. *Write a complete model business letter, illustrating arrangement, punctuation, composition, use of capitals, etc.*

[For the applicant.]

8. *Examiner will grade the penmanship of the answers to the above questions at forty per cent.*

THEORY AND PRACTICE.

GENERAL PEDAGOGICS AND METHODS.

[Wilkinson.]

1. *Outline the functions of education, and distinguish between formal and informal.*

Ans. The function of education is to develop the intellect; to correlate and perfect all the powers of man, the body with the mind, the mind with the soul, the perceptive faculties with the reflective, both of these with the feelings and reason, and all of these with the will; to enlarge, correct and harmonize the social, political and religious life of the individual, and to make the self more and more like the Infinite One, in whose image he is created. Formal education is development of the intellect by set tasks, the getting of knowledge, and formation of habit by assigned and prepared lessons in daily routine of work. Informal is that important education which comes from the exercise of self upon the play-ground; at home; in association with the teacher, fellow-pupils, and neighbors; the communion with nature, and the close fellowship with books,— the development of character which arises from example and influence.

2. *Give a clear definition of the art of teaching.*

Ans. Teaching is the art of feeding minds to make them grow, and of exercising minds to make them develop harmoniously and in due order and correlation.

3. *Discuss the sources of the child's information and the methods by which he confirms his ideas.*

Ans. Instinct and intuition, both of which are born with him, the former growing feebler and more uncertain as education progresses, the latter deepening and broadening with the processes of development; sensation, which brings all the knowledge of the outside world to the mind; reflection and reason, which add to, correlate, systematize and classify the knowledge received; emotions and will, which supply motive power, choice and control. The products of each of these mental activities are further added to from the experience and example of teacher and associates, and are confirmed by the logic of experience of himself and of others and from books.

4. *Distinguish between the unscientific and the scientific teacher.*

Ans. The former tries to impart knowledge without regard to the laws of the mind; its orderly development, the correlation of branches taught, or the idiosyncrasies of the particular child. The scientific teacher takes account of all these, and is continually studying each problem as it presents itself, adapting and inventing methods to meet the emergencies as they arise.

5. *Describe the characteristics of a good text-book, and explain how text-books should be used.*

Ans. (*a*) It should be lucid, simple and esthetic in its language and enunciation of principles. Its style should be the very best. Its arrangement of matter should be scholarly and scientific. Its type should be plain and clear-cut, upon good paper. None but the best illustrations should be used, and they should be as numerous as possible. It should be tastefully and durably bound.

(*b*) It should be used as an outline or guide, and not as final authority.

6. *Define memory, and show what methods the teacher may use to strengthen it.*

Ans. (*a*) Memory is defined by some as the faculty, by others as the condition, by which the mind records, retains and restores the ideas gained by its own activity.

(*b*) By establishing likeness, unlikeness, or connection in time or place with some other thing; by presenting important facts carefully discriminated from unimportant; by classifying and arranging facts; by allowing time for the matter to "soak in"; by repetition of ideas involved as well as of words in which the ideas are expressed.

7. *Discuss the effect of previous learning, association, occupation and modes of thought on each new act of learning.*

Ans. They are all important, since by previous learning the mind proceeds from the known to the unknown; association is necessary for right understanding, and occupation and modes of thought determine the quickness of apprehension, interest aroused, etc.

8. *What are the best methods of questioning?*

Ans. Those which will make the questioned one think, and thus bring to bear in answering the question all the knowledge and mental strength and energy at his command.

9. *How do you stimulate interest?*

Ans. By being interested, and by appealing to those phases of the matter which will enlist the self-interest and pleasure of the pupil.

10. *How are great skill and rapidity attained in the school arts?*

Ans. By securing a perfect mastery of the elements of the art, followed by frequent repetition in which two elements constantly enter into the task,—accuracy and time-limit.

THEORY AND PRACTICE.

ELEMENTARY EDUCATIONAL PSYCHOLOGY.

[Wilkinson.]

1. *Why is a knowledge of the nature of the child mind more important than that of the adult?*

Ans. Because the child is yet to be educated; his mind is to be developed, and his habits formed. The adult's education is practically complete, his mental activities have become fixed in certain directions, and his habits established.

2. *Show how the temperament and moods of the child are dependent upon his physical condition.*

Ans. Hunger, thirst, too high temperature, too low temperature, bad air, will make him restless, uneasy, cross, irritable, and stupid, from their reaction upon his nervous, respiratory and circulatory systems.

3. *Explain the intellectual, the esthetic and the practical value of the sense of hearing.*

Ans. It brings to the mind a great portion of knowledge of the outside world. It enables one to distinguish musical sounds, and, when properly educated, to appreciate the beauty in rustling leaves, running water, chirping insects, singing birds, the variety of delight in all instruments, and the matchless harmony of the human voice. This sense enables us to protect ourselves from approaching danger, as the approach of a train, the rattle of a snake, a cry of fire, and assures us help and protection when we call. It also enables us to communicate with our fellows, saving much time and loss of energy, etc.

4. *Explain what we mean by knowing a thing.*

Ans. When we come to understand it thoroughly in all its relations to other things so that it becomes a part of self, we are said to know a thing.

5. *Define feeling, and explain its relations to knowledge.*

Ans. (*a*) Feelings are agitations or impulses of the mind.

(*b*) The relation is so intimate that the mind is only moved by a thing in proportion to its knowledge of that thing. The principal factors in the growth of feeling are: memory, imagination, habit, and temperament.

6. *Distinguish between the emotional life of the child and that of the adult.*

Ans. A child's feelings are selfish and rudimentary, bound up with his bodily wants and the lower forms of sensation. They are limited by his intelligence, which is weak. They are non-representative, intense, violent, fugitive, and brief. The adult's feeling is more social, and consequently less selfish, and for sensations are substituted the sentiments or reflective feelings.

7. *Show by what processes perceptions result in conceptions.*

Ans. By observation or perception two or more individuals resembling one another in one or more particulars are brought together as percepts or images; these percepts or images are compared and contrasted by the mind, which pays special attention to the points of resemblance; the result of this special attention is to draw or abstract these resemblances from the differences; these abstracted resemblances thus grouped together form the concept; the concept becomes clearer in the mind, other individuals are noticed having qualities which agree with those of the concept, and gradually generalization, the idea of a certain class of things having these certain characteristics of the concept in common, is reached.

8. *Define judgment, and explain what becomes of the element of knowledge it furnishes.*

Ans. Judgment is the relation established between ideas. This establishment of relation between ideas becomes and is the essential that enters into the next higher mental operation, reasoning, which is the establishment of the relation between judgments.

9. *How do habits originate, and how are they related to knowledge?*

Ans. (*a*) Habit is a fixed tendency to think, feel or act in a particular way under special circumstances, and this tendency originates in the regularity and frequency with which the thought, feeling or act is repeated.

(*b*) By habit, conduct is rendered easy, thus economizing the effort of the will. The growth of the power of attention is the result of the growth of habit. Habit strengthens memory; forms concentration, repetition, and classification; fixes the habit of inquiry, which makes it necessary for reason, and lessens the narrowness of knowledge.

10. *What value do you place upon the knowledge of psychology for the teacher?*

Ans. The laws of the mind and its orderly development must from the nature of the case be the most important branch of study for the teacher. Without a knowledge of these a teacher will act blindly, not knowing how to detect and to remove defects peculiar to the young learner. Without them she may teach, but without them she can never educate.

PHYSIOLOGY.

[Spangler.]

1. *What is the function of the skin, and what glands does it contain?*

Ans. (*a*) The outer co ering and most important excretory organ of the body; the principal regulator of the body's temperature; a protector of the parts within, and a source of beauty and grace.

(*b*) It contains the sweat-glands, the sebaceous glands, and the absorbent tubes or lymphatics.

2. *Name all the organs that aid in excretion and their products.*

Ans. The lungs exhale carbon dioxide, watery vapor, and other waste matter in gaseous form; the large intestine secretes effete matters from the blood and expels them with the innutritious or waste portions of the aliment from the body; the kidneys excrete water and saline matter; the skin excretes carbon dioxide, water, saline matter, waste tissue (oil and fat), and other effete products.

3. *What are the main differences between the right and left sides of the heart?*

Ans. The muscular walls of the left side are thicker and stronger than are those of the right side. The valve between the right auricle and right ventricle has three leaflets, while that between the left auricle and ventricle has but two. The right side of the heart receives from the systematic circulation and gives to the pulmonary; while the left receives from the pulmonary circulationa and gives to the systematic.

4. *What ferments act upon starch, and where do they act? What kind of a medium?*

Ans. (*a*) Saliva, in the mouth; pancreatic juice and the intestinal juice, in the small intestine.

(*b*) An alkaline, chemical, watery-looking fluid secreted by the salivary glands and the intestinal glands.

5. *Describe the main cavities of the body, and name their linings.*

Ans. The skull, lined with the dura mater; the nasal cavity and the mouth, with mucous membrane; the thoracic, with pleura; the abdomen and pelvic, with the peritoneum; the spinal cavity, with the dura mater, protected by an enveloping cushion of fatty tissue.

6. *What is the difference between the dorsal and ventral nerve roots, and what is their function?*

Ans. This question must refer to the posterior and anterior roots of the spinal cord, which put off the former from the dorsal and the latter from the ventral side of the column. The dorsal is composed of gray matter, and is sensory, the ventral is made up of white matter, and is motor. The function of the dorsal or sensory nerve fibers is to convey sensations to the brain. The function of the ventral or sensory nerve is to transmit motor impulses from the brain.

7. *Where is the medulla? What sensory nerves do not arise from it?*

Ans. (*a*) An enlargement or bulb which forms the upper extremity of the spinal cord. It is situated within the skull, is continuous with the brain, and its gray matter occupies the interior.

(*b*) The first five pairs.

8. *How is bone tissue renewed? What is a fracture, dislocation, and bronchitis?*

Ans. (*a*) From the periosteum, through which ramify the blood-vessels which supply nourishment to the bone.

(*b*) When the bone is broken, the break is called a fracture.

(*c*) The separation of the extremities of bones that form a joint.

(*d*) An inflammation of the bronchial tubes.

9. *What is haemoglobin? glycogen? urea?*

Ans. (*a*) The coloring-matter of the blood, which contains a considerable proportion of iron oxide.

(*b*) A white amorphous, tasteless substance resembling starch, soluble in water, and found in the liver and other organs and tissues.

(*c*) A soluble crystalline body, which is the chief constituent of the urine, and is also found in the blood, liver, lymph, etc., in small quantities.

10. ***Where is the larynx, and what is its use? What diseased conditions are produced by immoderate use of alcohol?***

Ans. (*a*) The voice-box. It is the enlarged upper part of the air passage leading from the lungs to the base of the tongue. To frame and utter articulate speech.

(*b*) It shuts off air from the lungs by its effects upon lung tissue; withdraws water from the muscles and other tissues of the larynx, producing dryness, huskiness and paralysis of the vocal cords, and originates inflammation of the tissues and thickening and hardening of the cords.

CONSTITUTION.

[Massey.]

1. ***How may a bill become a law? How may it be lost?***

Ans. (*a*) By receiving a majority vote of the members elected in each house and the signature of the president; by receiving a majority vote of the members elected in each house more than ten days (Sundays excepted) before a session adjourns, and being retained by the president without his signature; by receiving a majority vote of all the members elected in each house, being vetoed by the president, and passed over his veto by a two-thirds vote in each house.

(*b*) By failing to receive a majority vote in either of the houses; by receiving a majority vote in each house within ten days (Sundays excepted) of the session adjourning and being kept by the president without his signature; by failure of president to sign and no action being taken in relation thereto by the houses; by refusal of president to sign, and thereupon failing to receive the necessary two-thirds vote in either house to override the veto.

2. ***Give ten absolute prohibitions on States.***

Ans. No State shall—

(*a*) Enter into any alliance, treaty, or confederation.

(*b*) Grant letters of marque and reprisal.

(*c*) Coin money.

(*d*) Emit bills of credit.

(*e*) Make anything but gold or silver coin a tender in payment of debts.

(*f*) Pass any bill of attainder, *ex post facto* law, or law impairing the obligation of contract.

(*g*) Grant any title of nobility.

(*h*) Impose slavery or involuntary servitude except where party shall have been convicted of crime.

(*i*) Make or enforce any law which shall abridge the privileges or immunities of citizens of the United States; nor deprive any person of the equal protection of the laws, nor of life, liberty or property without due process of law.

(*j*) Deny or abridge the right of any citizen of the United States to vote on account of race, color, or previous condition of servitude.

3. *Give name of officer at the head of each department of the Government.*

Ans. Secretary of State, John Hay; Secretary of Treasury, Lyman J. Gage; Secretary of War, Elihu Root; Attorney-General, P. C. Knox; Postmaster-General, Chas. E. Smith; Secretary of Navy, John D. Long; Secretary of Interior, Ethan A. Hitchcock; Secretary of Agriculture, James Wilson.

4. *Explain different processes by which the State may take property from a citizen.*

Ans. By right of eminent domain, by necessity in time of war, by condemnation for public use. In all these cases compensation must be rendered for the property taken. By judgment in court of law, and to prevent the commission of a crime.

5. *What constitute the supreme law of the land, and how may each cease to be such?*

Ans. The constitution, by amendment of particular sections; treaties, by expiration of time for which made, or by acts of repeal, such as a formal declaration, a war, etc.; statutes of the United States, by special amendment or repeal by Congress.

6. *Give ten provisions of the constitution to secure personal liberty.*

Ans. (*a*) There shall be no State religion.

(*b*) The exercise of religion shall be free.

(*c*) Freedom of speech is guaranteed.

(*d*) The right to assemble and petition for redress of grievances is assured.

(*e*) The right to keep and bear arms is confirmed.

(*f*) Security in person, house, papers and effects against unreasonable searches and seizures.

(*g*) Indictment or presentment of a grand jury necessary to hold a person for a capital or otherwise infamous crime.

(*h*) Cannot be twice put in jeopardy for the same offense.

(*i*) When charged with crime the accused has right to a

speedy and public trial, by an impartial jury of the State and district wherein the crime shall have been committed, and be informed of the nature and cause of the accusation; be confronted with witnesses against him; have compulsory process for obtaining witnesses in his own behalf; and to have the assistance of counsel for his defense.

(*j*) Excessive bail, excessive fines and cruel and unusual punishments are prohibited.

7. *Locate each of the State institutions.*

Ans. State University, at Lawrence; State Agricultural College, Manhattan; State Normal School, Emporia; Boys' Industrial School, Topeka; Girls' Industrial School, Beloit; Industrial Reformatory (for men), Hutchinson; School for Feeble-Minded Youth, Winfield; School for the Blind, Kansas City; School for the Deaf and Dumb, Olathe; Hospitals for Insane, Topeka and Osawatomie; Soldiers' Orphans' Home, Atchison; State Penitentiary, Lansing.

8. *Describe briefly the ceremony of introduction of our ambassadors at foreign courts.*

Ans. Upon arriving at his post the minister calls upon the minister of foreign affairs. After introduction he presents a certified copy of his credentials, and a draft of the address he intends to deliver to the sovereign at his presentation. The minister of foreign affairs fixes a time for the official presentation, and hands the minister a copy of the address the sovereign intends to make on that occasion. These copies of the addresses are interchanged, so that anything offensive may be stricken out before delivery. At the time appointed, the minister is waited upon at his legation by the official "introducer of ambassadors," and attended by that gentleman he proceeds to the sovereign's palace. There he meets the minister of foreign affairs, who escorts him to the door of the throne-room. Upon the door being thrown open, he sees the sovereign seated on his throne at the opposite end of the room. With the "introducer of ambassadors" upon his left, the minister of foreign affairs at his right, and his secretaries behind him, he makes a low bow. The whole party with slow and dignified steps advance to the center of the room, stop, and bow again. They resume their march until a respectful distance from the throne is reached, where they stop, and bow a third time. The "introducer" then announces the minister's name, "envoy extraordinary and minister plenipotentiary from the United States." The presented minister reads his address, and hands to the minister of foreign affairs his credentials, which are passed up to the sovereign and received by some attendant. The sovereign then reads his address, and, generally, at its conclusion, descends from the throne, offers his hand to the new minister and presents him to the royal consort, and other members of the court, which terminates the presentation. The minister and his escort bow, retire backward to the center of the room, bow again, and continue to retire until the door is reached, where, after the third bow, they turn and walk naturally. The sovereign is attired in his robes of state, all his court and other ambassadors in gold-laced uniforms, with ribbons and decorations. The United States minister appears in plain evening dress. Within twenty-four hours he must call upon the minister of foreign affairs and other members of the cabinet, and the other members of the diplomatic corps.

9. *What action did President Cleveland take in the settlement of the Venezuelan trouble?*

Ans. During 1895, the boundary dispute between Great Britain and Venezuela called for a reaffirmance of the Monroe Doctrine. President Cleveland informed England, "the established policy of the United States is against a forcible increase of any territory of a European power" in the New World, and she "is bound to protest against the enlargement of the area of British Guiana against the will of Venezuela"; and invited England to submit to arbitration. England refused arbitration, and denied that the Monroe Doctrine was applicable "to the state of things in which we live to-day." The President then asked from Congress the authority to appoint a commission to examine the boundary and report, declaring that the United States would be bound by the report to support such claims of Venezuela as the report found just and right. November 12, 1896, England and Venezuela signed a treaty of arbitration at Washington.

10. *How do the salaries of our diplomatic agents compare with those of the leading powers of Europe? Give some specific illustrations.*

Ans. (*a*) They are much less than those paid by any other great power.

(*b*) Our ambassadors to England, France, Germany, Russia, and Mexico, each receive $17,500 annually. The British minister to the United States receives $50,000 per year, his residence, horses and carriages, and a number of servants. In addition, the minister from the United States has less assistance than is granted to their ministers by other governments. For instance, Mexico's minister to our country has six secretaries, while our minister to that country has but one.

PHYSICS.

[Spangler.]

1. *How far will a body fall in three seconds?*

Ans. The space passed over by a body falling freely in any given number of seconds is equal to the space described in the first second (16.08 feet) multiplied by the square of the number of seconds.

$$9 \times 16.08 = 144.72 \text{ feet.}$$

2. *What is meant by the mass of a body? How is it measured?*

Ans. (*a*) The amount of matter a body contains irrespective of its bulk or volume.

(*b*) By multiplying together its density and volume. Generally, it is used interchangeably with weight, since weight is proportional to mass; but weight is the measure of the comparative force that attracts the mass to the center of the earth.

3. *A body weighs 10 grams in air and 8 grams in water; what is its specific gravity?*

Ans. Specific gravity = weight of equal volume of substance ÷ weight of equal volume of water. The loss in weight is the weight of equal volume of water. Then we have:

$x = \frac{10}{2}$

$x = 5$, specific gravity of substance.

4. *What is the dew point?*

Ans. If air saturated with moisture is cooled, a portion of the moisture will be deposited as dew. The temperature at which this deposit occurs is called the dew point?

5. *What is heat? temperature? What is the centigrade scale?*

Ans. (*a*) That mode of molecular motion which may be measured by the expansion of matter.

(*b*) Intensity of heat referred to some arbitrary standard.

(*c*) A scale suggested by Celsius, in which zero is the st-rting-point, marking the temperature of water at point of becoming a solid, and the distance between zero and boiling water is divided into 100 equal parts; hence its name, Centigrade.

6. *On what does the color of a light depend?*

Ans. On the character of the matter, where it originates, and the degree of heat to which that matter is subjected; on the character of the medium which transmits it; on the character of the lens or prism, etc., through which it is viewed. Of course, the first in a philosophical sense is the only condition which can establish the color of a light.

7. *Explain the principle of a convex lens.*

Ans. Light passing from a rarer to a denser medium is bent toward the perpendicular; in passing from a denser to a rarer, from the perpendicular. The light is thus refracted twice toward the axis of the lens, and the several pencils are brought together at a point on the axis called the principal focus.

8. *If a current of 10 amperes flow through a resistance of 15 ohms, how much energy is transformed into heat?*

Ans. Current or amperage $= \frac{\text{voltage}}{\text{ohmage}}$

$$10 = \frac{x}{15}$$

Voltage = 150 = 150 watts of energy, or $\frac{150}{746}$ H. P.

BOOKKEEPING.

[Bushey.]

June 8. Began business with cash $500; merchandise, 2000 bu. oats, at thirty cents.

9. Bought on account, of J. B. Jackson, 500 lbs. sugar, at four cents.

10. Bought for cash, 100 bbls. flour, at $3.90.

11. Sold to R. E. Weeks, on account, 1000 bu. oats, at forty cents.

12. Sold to T. T. Towne, far cash, 300 lbs. sugar, at six cents; 500 bu. oats, at forty-two cents.

13. Sold to W. B. Sands, 80 bbls. flour, at $4.60. Received payment draft at thirty days' sight on First National Bank, which they have accepted this day.

14. Paid store rent in cash, $20.

State inventory.

Journalize; post; make balance sheet.

JOURNAL. June 8, 1901.

	Account	Dr.	Cr.
	Cash	$500	
	Mdse	600	
	James Jamison		$1,100

9			
Mdse.		20	
J. B. Jackson			20
10			
Mdse		390	
Cash			390
11			
R. E. Weeks		400	
Mdse			400
12			
Cash		228	
Mdse			228
13			
Bills receivable		368	
Mdse			368
14			
Expense		20	
Cash			20
INVENTORY.			
500 bu. oats	@ 30	150	
20 bbls. flour	@ 3 90	78	
200 lbs. sugar	@ 04	8	
			236

Ledger.

James Jamison, Proprietor.

				June	8		$1,100

Cash.

June	8		$500	June	10		$390
June	12		228				20

Merchandise.

June	8		$600	June	11		$400
June	9		20	June	12		228
June	10		390	June	13		368

J. B. Jackson.

				June	9		$20

R. E. Weeks.

June	11		$400				

Bills Receivable.

June	13		$368				

Expense.

June	14			$20					

Balance Sheet.

James Jamison.......		$1,100				
Cash	$728	410			$318	
Mdse.................	1,010	996		$222	236	
J. B. Jackson.........		20				$20
R. E. Weeks	400				400	
Bills Receivable......	368				368	
Expense..............	20		$20			
	$2,526	$2,526	$20	$222	$1,322	$20
Gain			*202*			
Net Gain	$202					
Net Credit............	1,100					
Present Capital.......						1,302
					$1,322	$1,322

Monday and Tuesday, August 26 and 27, 1901.

ARITHMETIC.

[Nichols.]

1. *Simplify the following, and then reduce to a decimal, carrying to four places:*

$$\frac{\frac{2}{3}+3\frac{1}{2}}{1\frac{7}{8}-\frac{5}{12}}$$

Ans. $$\frac{\frac{2}{3}+3\frac{1}{2}}{1\frac{7}{8}-\frac{5}{12}}=\frac{16+84}{45+10}=\frac{100}{35}=2\frac{6}{7}=2.8571+$$

Note.—Multiply both terms of the fraction by 24, the L. C. M. of the small denominators, before performing the other operations.

2. *Reduce five-sevenths ton to lower denominations.*

Ans. $\frac{5}{7}$ T. $=\frac{5}{7}\times 20$ cwt. $=14\frac{2}{7}$ cwt.
$\frac{2}{7}$ cwt. $=\frac{2}{7}\times 100$ lbs. $=28\frac{4}{7}$ lbs.
$\frac{4}{7}$ lbs. $=\frac{4}{7}\times 16$ oz. $=9\frac{1}{7}$ oz.
$\frac{1}{7}$ oz. $=\frac{1}{7}\times 16$ dr. $=2\frac{2}{7}$ dr.
$\therefore$ $\frac{5}{7}$ T. $=14$ cwt. 28 lbs. 9 oz. $2\frac{2}{7}$ dr.

3. *Find the cost of papering the walls and ceiling of a room 9 feet by 12 feet and 10 feet high with paper one-half yard wide, at 20 cents per roll of 24 feet, no allowance being made for doors or windows or for matching.*

Ans. Perimeter of room = 42 ft. No. strips on sides = $\frac{42}{1\frac{1}{2}}=28$. One roll will make two strips, as pieces of strips are not used. No. rolls for sides = $\frac{28}{2}$, or 14. The more economical way is to run the ceiling strips lengthwise of the room. No. strips on the ceiling = 6. No. rolls on the ceiling = $\frac{6}{2}=3$. No. rolls required = 17.
Cost = 17 × 20¢ = $3.40.

4. *Find the present worth of a note for $8500 due in three months; interest at 8 per cent.*

Ans. 100% P. = present worth
2% P. = true discount
102% P. = face of note.
$\therefore$ 102% P. = $8500.
P. = $\frac{\$8500}{1.02}$ = 8333\frac{1}{3}$

5. *How many bushels of wheat can be placed, without heaping, in a bin 8 feet by 10 feet by 5 feet.*

Ans. No. bushels $= \frac{8 \times 10 \times 5 \times 1728}{2150.4} = 321.4+$

6. *After marking a certain piece of goods a dealer throws off 10 per cent. If a purchaser who receives an added discount of 4 per cent. for cash pays $21.60 for the piece, what was the first marked price?*

Ans. 96% of discounted price = $21.60.

Discounted price $= \frac{\$21.60}{.96} = \$22.50.$

90% of marked price = $22.50.

Marked price $= \frac{\$22.50}{.9} = \$25.$

7. *What are the names of the three tables of weight? State for what kind of goods each is made. Which weight is the same in all tables? Reduce one ounce avoirdupois to troy weight.*

Ans. Avoirdupois, Troy, and Apothecaries'.

Avoirdupois weight is used in weighing ordinary articles, as grains, fruits, vegetables, coal, etc.

Troy weight is used in weighing precious metals and precious stones.

Apothecaries' weight is used in weighing medicines.

The grain is the same in all.

One oz. Avoir. = 437½ gr. = 18 pwt. 5½ gr.

8. *Find the interest at 6 per cent. on $3765 from June 9, 1897, to August 4, 1898.*

Ans. Subtracting dates we have,

Time = 1 yr. 1 mo. 25 days.

$$\begin{array}{r} .06 \\ .005 \\ .004\frac{1}{6} \\ \hline \$.069\frac{1}{6} \end{array} = \text{interest on } \$1.$$

The interest on $3765 is 3765 times $.069⅙, or $260.41+

9. *What is the length of a side of a square 20-acre field? Carry the result to three decimal places.*

Ans. No. sq. rds. $= 20 \times 160 = 3200.$

No. rds. on a side $= \sqrt{3200.}$

$= 56.568+.$

10. *A woolen manufacturer sends his agent $2100 to invest in wool after deducting 5 per cent. commission. What is the purchase-price and what the commission?*

Ans. 100% P. = purchase price.

5% P. = commission.

105% P. = cost.

$\therefore 105\%$ P. = \$2100.

P. = $\frac{\$2100}{1.05}$ = \$2000.

Commission = \$100.

GRAMMAR.

[Bushey.]

(1) "What think you," said Washington;
(2) "If we should retreat to the back
(3) parts of Pennsylvania, would the
(4) Pennsylvanians support us?"

1. *Point out the principal clause in the above sentence.*

Ans. "Said Washington."

2. *Give the construction of the word* WHAT *(line 1).*

Ans. Objective case, object of "think."

3. *What does the clause,* IF WE SHOULD RETREAT, *etc., (line 2) modify?*

Ans. If the question means the clause ending with the word, "Pennsylvania," the clause modifies "would support."

Let us rejoice that neither of them threatens to return to vex either the soil of the West or the soul of our government.

4. *Give the construction of* REJOICE *in the above sentence.*

Ans. "Us [to] rejoice" is an objective noun phrase, object of "let," of which "us" is the subject of the infinitive "[to] rejoice."

5. *Give construction of* TO VEX *in above sentence.*

Ans. An adverbial phrase of purpose, modifying "to return."

6. *Give the construction of the clause,* THAT NEITHER OF THEM THREATENS, *etc.*

Ans. Adverbial clause modifying "[to] rejoice."

7. *Give construction of* US *in above sentence.*

Ans. Part of the object of "let" and the subject of the infinitive "[to] rejoice."

8. *Write a sentence illustrating a clause used in apposition with a noun or pronoun.*

Ans. He repeated the hackneyed expression, "All men are mortal."

9. *Give a synopsis of the verb* SUPPORT *in the passive voice, indicative mode, third person, singular.*

Ans.

Present.	*Present Perfect.*
Is supported.	Has been supported.
Past.	*Past Perfect.*
Was supported.	Had been supported.
Future.	*Future Perfect.*
Will be supported.	Will have been supported.

10. *Write a sentence containing an adjective used appositively.*

Ans. You, young and vigorous,—how can you fail?

GEOGRAPHY.

[Nelson.]

1. *How would you teach the points of the compass to a primary class?*

Ans. By establishing the four cardinal points from facing the sunrise quarter; left hand, north; right hand, south; back, west. Then establish the direction of houses, trees and natural features in relation to the school-house.

2. *Explain how you would develop in a child's mind the idea of a mountain range; an ocean; a continent.*

Ans. By reference to hills or large bodies of water, if any, surrounding, and to land stretching away in every direction; by use of sand-map building, relief maps, personal experiences of children, descriptions.

3. *Define latitude, longitude. Show how you would teach these to a class.*

Ans. (*a*) Distance north or south of the equator.

(*b*) Distance east or west of a given meridian.

(*c*) By demonstration upon a blackboard, globe, or ordinary globe, or upon the map, upon a ball or apple, and upon the blackboard.

4. *Compare Rocky Mountains and Alleghany mountains as to direction, length, width, and elevations of plateaus and valley.*

Ans. The former extend from northwest to southeast; from 7½° N. Lat. to Arctic Circle, have an average width of 10° of longitude, and are characterized by lofty plateaus, deep canyons, and extensive basins. The latter trend from northeast to southwest from 32° to 47° N. Lat.; have an average width of about 5° Long.; plateaus are broad, but not of great altitude, and valleys and foot-hills are numerous and fertile.

5. *Compare North America and South America as to climate, soils, products, and people.*

Ans. (*a*) Only a small part of North America is in the hot and cold belts. Much the greater part has cold or cool winters and hot or warm summers. In the warm belt the winter is short and mild, but northward it lengthens, until in the extreme north coldness and dreariness characterize the entire year. The equatorial rains of summer reach only the extreme southern parts. The north and middle regions of South America are in the trade-wind belts, and have frequent rains, and the equatorial rain belt shifts north and south across the northern half. The southern part of the continent extends far into the cold belt in the path of the stormy westerly winds.

(*b*) In the north part of North America are vast cold plains which do not yield much; south of these are stretches of wooded plains; and south of these are the dry plains, the prairies, and the Mississippi Valley—all of which are fertile; in the Rockies and Alleghanies are fertile valleys, and the costal plains of the Atlantic, Pacific and Gulf of Mexico are very rich. Mexico and Central America have a soil that yields in richest abundance all kinds of semi-tropical fruits and products. South America has a very narrow strip of farm-land west of the Andes; in the north are vast alluvial tracts, the rich forest plains of the Amazon, and south of these stretch the great fertile grass lands.

(*c*) North America has all the products of the Frigid Zone, of the North Temperate, of the Semi-tropical regions, and some of the Tropical belt. South America has all those of the Tropical, Semi-tropical, and South Temperate.

(*d*) In the north, North America has the Esquimax and Indians, farther south the plain and mountain Indians and the Mexican aborigines. It is settled mainly by English, Scotch, Irish, Germans, Swedes, Dutch and French emigrants and their descendants from Europe, and in the south by Spanish. South America has in addition to her aborigines (the Incas of Peru, and Indians of the North, and the Patagonians and Fuegians) a population from Europe made up in the main of Spanish and Portuguese.

6. *What part of the western slope of the Andes is arid? What part of it has a moist climate? Why?*

Ans. (*a*) More than a thousand miles along the west slope of the middle Andes.

(*b*) The southern Andes and the extreme northern Andes slopes.

(*c*) The rainless region of the middle Andes is too near the equator to receive the storms of the westerly winds, and too remote to receive the rains from the shifting equatorial belt. The extreme northern Andes receive the equatorial rains, and the southern Andes receive the rains brought by the westerly winds during the winter.

7. *How does the structure of Africa differ from that of all the other continents?*

Ans. It is rounded in outline, having few bays, and almost the entire continent is a highland. Its costal plains are narrow, because the border ranges of the highland are near the sea, and almost all the inland is a plateau. It has a wide forest belt in the equatorial region. On both sides of this belt are grass plains, beyond which are vast deserts.

8. *What causes winds? ocean currents?*

Ans (*a*) Movements of the atmosphere produced by unequal heating of the different parts of the earth, elevations of surface, etc.

(*b*) Movements of oceanic waters—produced in the same manner as winds and modified by depth and expanse of waters, configuration of shores, etc.

9. *Locate five capes, five lakes and five large cities of North America.*

Ans. (*a*) Point Barrow, northern extremity of Alaska; Prince of Wales, westernmost cape of Alaska; Mendocino, western United States; St. Lucas, southern extremity of Lower California; Hatteras, eastern United States.

(*b*) Great Bear and Great Slave Lakes in northwestern Canada; Winnipeg, southern Canada; Great Salt Lake, western United States; Superior, Huron, Erie and Ontario, between Canada and the United States; and Michigan, northern United States.

(*c*) New York, northeastern United States, at mouth of Hudson river; Chicago, northeast central United States, on Lake Michigan; Philadelphia, northeastern United States, at junction of Delaware and Schuylkill rivers; Boston, northeastern United States, on Massachusetts bay; Mexico, south of center of Mexico.

10. *Locate Manila, Porto Rico, Berlin, Montreal, Klondike, Guam, Cape Nome, Buenos Ayres.*

Ans. (*a*) Capital of Luzon, Philippine Islands.

(*b*) One of United States islands, southeast of Florida.

(*c*) Capital of German Empire, in Prussia.

(*d*) City of southeastern Canada, on St. Lawrence river.

(*e*) Gold region, in eastern Alaska and northeastern Canada.

(*f*) One of the United States' islands, situated in the Pacific, about 25° east of the Philippines.

(*g*) Cape in gold region, western coast of Alaska.

(*h*) Capital and province of the Argentine Confederation. The capital is in the northeastern part of the province, o the Rio de la Plata river.

UNITED STATES HISTORY.

[Riggs.]

1. *Sketch the voyages and discoveries of the Northmen.*

Ans. There is reason to believe that about the year 1000, A. D., Leif Ericson sailed from Iceland to make his father, Eric the Red, who had previously settled in Greenland, a visit. Leif either lost his way or was driven by storms to the southward until he reached an unknown land which he called Vinland, on account of the profusion of grapes found there. Precisely where Vinland was is not known, but it was certainly a part of North America, for, leaving there, Leif sailed north to Greenland.

2. *With what events are the names of Frobisher, Davis, Gilbert, Drake and Gosnold connected, respectively?*

Ans. (*a*) In 1576, Sir Martin Frobisher, in trying to find the northwest passage to Asia, explored our coasts and gave his name to Frobisher's Bay.

(*b*) In 1587, Davis, in the same attempt, discovered and explored Davis Strait, which separates Greenland from the main land.

(*c*) In 1579, under a charter from Queen Elizabeth, Sir Humphrey Gilbert attempted to found a colony, but failed. and while sailng home from Newfoundland, 1583, he and his crew were lost in a storm at sea.

(*d*) In 1577, Sir Francis Drake sailed down the eastern South-American coast, doubled the cape, sailed up the west coast of South America, and as far north as Oregon, in search of a northeast passage to the Atlantic. Warned by the growing cold and the disquiet of his men, he turned south, landed at the present site of San Francisco in June, 1579, nailed to a post a brass plate bearing the name of Queen Elizabeth, and took possession in her name; crossed the Pacific, rounded Cape Good Hope and reached England, having sailed around the world.

(e) Bartholomew Gosnold, in 1602, landed at and explored the shores of Cape Cod, in Massachusetts.

3. *What was the reason for the establishment of Mason and Dixon's line, and where is it?*

Ans. There was a long dispute between Penn and Lord Baltimore and their successors over the boundary between Pennsylvania and Maryland, which was not settled until a survey of adjustment was made in 1763-1767 by Charles Mason and Jeremiah Dixon, and this boundary was located as well as those of Delaware as they now are. In later years, when the Atlantic seaboard States north of Maryland and Delaware had abolished slavery, this "Mason and Dixon's Line" became noted as the dividing line between free States and slave States.

4. *How many men were in Washington's first cabinet, and what positions did they hold?*

Ans. Three: Secretary of State, Thomas Jefferson; Secretary of the Treasury, Alexander Hamilton; Secretary of War, General Henry Knox.

5. *What were the alien and sedition laws?*

Ans. Laws passed by the Federalists during President John Adams's administration. The Alien Law extended the term of residence before naturalization to nine years, and gave the President power for two years to send any alien out of the country whenever he thought proper to do so. The Sedition Law provided that any one interfering with the execution of a law of Congress, or abusing the President, or Congress, or any member of the Federal Government, should on conviction be fined and imprisoned.

6. *Discuss the Dred Scott decision and its results.*

Ans. The "Dred Scott Decision" was an opinion rendered by the Supreme Court of the United States March 6, 1857, holding, in brief:

1. That a negro whose ancestors had been sold as slaves could not become a citizen of the United States, nor of any State, and could not sue in the United States courts.

2. That such described negro was a slave, and that, as a slave, he was property, a chattel, as a horse or cow.

3. That Congress could not exclude him from the Territories any more than it could any kind of property, as a horse or cow.

4. That the Missouri Compromise of 1820 was null and void.

This confirmed the Kansas-Nebraska Act of 1854, and opened to slavery all the Territories which were free. This decision made the slave party reckless in its delight; split the Democratic party in the North; increased the Republican party in the North and made it more definitely a free party; and assisted in bringing about the election of President Lincoln.

7. *Describe Farragut's capture of New Orleans.*

Ans. New Orleans was defended by two strong forts, opposite each other, on the Mississippi river, about seventy-five miles south of New Orleans; by two great chain cables stretched across the river below the forts, to prevent ships coming up; and by fifteen armored ships above the forts. Coming up as far as the chains, Farragut bombarded the forts for six days and nights. He then cut the chains, ran his fleet past the forts (April 24, 1862), destroyed the rebel fleet the next day, and took the city.

8. *What are the present relations between the United States and Cuba?*

Ans. Cuba is under the protection and control of the United States until she shall have adopted and put in motion a free, republican government, under a constitution ratified by the people of Cuba.

9. *What are the advantages and disadvantages of party fusion?*

Ans. The only advantage is the union of forces against a common political foe. The disadvantages are the necessity of supporting principles and policies to which many of the voters of the combine do not give their adherence, and quarrels over the distribution of the spoils if victorious, and over the policies that shall be advocated by the combine in the future.

10. *Give, in brief, the story of the capitals of Kansas.*

Ans. For fifty days Fort Leavenworth was Kansas' first capital city. On Nov. 24, 1854, Governor Reeder moved the seat of government to the Shawnee Manual Labor School, Shawnee Mission, in Johnson county, seven miles from Kansas City, Mo. April 14, 1855, he convened the Legislature at Pawnee, near Fort Riley. The Legislature refused to remain at Pawnee, and relocated at Shawnee Mission. In August, 1855, the Legislature located the capital at Lecompton, and here the second Legislature transacted its business. But the third and every succeeding Legislature until 1861 met first at Lecompton and then promptly adjourned to Lawrence. The first Legislature of the State met in Topeka, the then temporary capital, which soon after became the permanent seat of government.

READING.

[Massey.]

1. (a) *Name and define three methods of teaching beginners to read.* (b) *Give two arguments in favor of the one which you prefer.*

Ans. (*a*) Alphabet method teaches familiarity with the letters before combining them into words.

Word method teaches the word as a whole without reference especially to the letters of which it is composed.

Sentence method teaches the sentence as a whole without first rquiring a mastery of the individual words composing the sentence.

(*b*) The electic method, which combines the alphabet and word method seems best to the writer:

1. Because the child-mind becomes confused in attempting to master at once so many unfamiliar words as are united in the sentence.

2. Because, if he does not know something of the individual letters, he will be confused by words that vary only in one or two letters.

2. *Define ten technical terms used in reading.*

Ans. Emphasis, particular stress of voice laid upon a particular word or phrase.

Accent, stress upon a particular syllable of a word.

Inflection, the upward, downward or sustained modulation of the voice.

Gesture, movements of the hands, feet, head or other parts of the body to assist in the interpretation of the thought.

Rhetorical Pause, a pause made for the purpose of more effectively illustrating the meaning.

Pitch, the point upon the musical scale assumed by the voice.

Force, the energy used in uttering the words.

Quality, the peculiar attribute given the sound by the place of resonance, as in the chest, throat, mouth, etc.

Expression, the changes in pitch, force, quality, etc., of the voice to accord with the character of the thought and emotions being interpreted.

Rate, the speed or degree of rapidity with which the words are uttered.

3. *How can you create a love of nature in connection with our elementary reading-books?*

Ans. By calling upon and encouraging the children to observe the animals and plants about them, and to report their observations in connection with the lesson; by supplementing their work with natural objects collected by them and the teacher, and conversing with them about those objects, and by reading to them and causing them to read appreciative descriptions written in language that they can comprehend.

4. *Name the physical and the mental qualifications of a good reader.*

Ans. The teacher should be sound in every part, with no bodily ailments or drawbacks. She should have a mind well stocked with information, which she can command in expression at any moment; knowledge of the child-mind and its development; knowledge derived from careful study of the idiosyncrasies of the individual pupils; exemplary habits of speech and deportment; a love and a sympathy for humanity. She should be good-natured, just, patient, and of the highest Christian character. In short, she should have not only a sound body but an excellently "sound mind in a sound body."

5. *How can you teach a chart class a knowledge of the elementary sounds?*

Ans. By practicing the class individually and in concert upon the several sounds as they appear upon the chart and in word combinations. By constant daily review and drill upon the sounds.

6-10. *Write ten pertinent class questions on the following poem:*

1. All things bright and beautiful,
   All creatures, great and small,
 All things wise and wonderful—
   The Lord God made them all.

2. Each little flower that opens,
 Each little bird that sings—
He made their glowing colors,
 He made their tiny wings.

3. The purple-headed mountain,
 The river running by,
The morning and the sunset,
 That lighted up the sky.

4. The tall trees in the greenwood,
 The pleasant summer sun,
The ripe fruits in the garden—
 He made them every one.

5. He gave us eyes to see them,
 And lips that we might tell
How great is God Almighty
 Who hath made all things well.

—*Student's Third Reader.*

Ans. What is the difference between "things" and "creatures" in the first stanza?

In what respect, if any, does the second "things" differ from the first in meaning?

To what does "colors" in the second stanza refer?

What are the respective antecedents of the two "theirs" that occur in the second stanza, and why are these pronouns plural?

Do mountains have purple heads? Explain about the color purple.

Does the sunset add light to the sky? If it does, why is there a comma after sunset?

Give the case and construction of "creatures" in the first, "bird" in the second, "river" in the third, and "fruits" in the fourth stanza.

Independent of the thought involved, do you consider the selection an example of good poetry? Why?

ORTHOGRAPHY.

[Riggs.]

1. *Define* ORTHOGRAPHY, ORTHOEPY, ELEMENTARY SOUND, COMPOUND, INITIAL, *and* FINAL.

Ans. (*a*) The art or practice of writing or speaking words with the proper letters according to standard uses.

(*b*) The art of pronouncing words correctly.

(*c*) One produced by a single impulse of the vocal organs.

(*d*) A word made up of two of more words joined together by a hyphen.

(*e*) The first or beginning letter of a word or syllable.

(*f*) The last or closing letter of a word or syllable. Initial and final are also sometimes used in distinguishing between the first and last syllables of a word.

2. *Use in words the following prefixes or modifications of them, and define each word so as to bring out the meaning of the prefix:* A, DE, PRE, HYPER, RE, SYN, TRANS, OB.

Ans. *a*, afoot, *on* foot; *de*, debark, *from* a bark or vessel; *pre*, prefix, to fix *before; hyper*, hypercritical, *over* critical; *re*, recall, to call *back; syn*, synopsis, a view *together; trans*, transform, to form *through and through; ob*, obstacle, something standing *before* or *against*.

3. *Give the vocal and the aspirate consonant sounds of the language.*

Ans. The vocal or sonant consonants, are: b, d, j, g, w, v, th(y), r, z, zh, y, l, m, n, ng.

The aspirate or surd consonants are: p, t, ch, k, h, f, th(in), s, sh.

4. *Give the substitutes for the sound of* E *in* HER, *and use each substitute in a word where it represents the sound.*

Ans. There is considerable diversity about this sound. Perhaps the majority of English-speaking people accept as substitutes *e* in her, *i* in sir, *ea* in earn, *y* in myrtle, *ue* in guerdon.

5. *What are synonyms, antonyms, and homonyms? Give examples of each.*

Ans. (*a*) One of two or more words which have very nearly the same signification, and therefore may often be used interchangeably; thus, in *force* of mind and *strength* of mind, *force* and *strength* are synonyms.

(*b*) Two words of opposite meanings are antonyms, as *life* to *death*, *good* to *evil*.

(*c*) Words pronounced alike are homonyms; as, *cite, site, sight*.

6-10. *Spell correctly: acommodate, controler, gauge, numonia, liquorish, sargent, erassible, oxigen, thoracic, parallelogram, prellat, chapple, munisiple, Portugeese, metonomy, auxilary, manufactury, philiment, billy-doo, trooso, separate, asma, yoman, edible, indispensible.*

[See any dictionary.—ED.]

PENMANSHIP.

[Wilkinson.]

1. *What training in penmanship have you had?*

[For the applicant.]

2. *Have you practiced slant or vertical writing, or both?*

[For the applicant.]

3. *Describe the position for writing you would require your pupils to assume.*

Ans. In general, I require a square front position of the body, so that both arms may be placed on the desk. Where two pupils sit at one desk it may be necessary to sit with the right side to the desk, the body fronting at an angle of 45 deg. with the desk. In this case, it requires constant vigilance on the part of the teacher to prohibit the pupil from acquiring a crooked shape of the body while writing. Too much stress cannot be placed on the necessity of a position that is easy and firm,—a position with both feet flat on the floor and directly in front of the body, and the muscles of the body, arms and hand as free as possible from contortions of any kind.

4. *What are the essentials of good writing?*

Ans. The essentials of good writing are: First, a legible style of script, that can be executed continuously. Second, a manner of movement that makes the writing smooth and regular. Third, an established hand, which the writer may claim for his own.

5. *Is slant necessary to rapid writing? Give your reason for your answer.*

Ans. Slant is not necessary to rapid writing. While it may appear that slant writing may be executed more easily, it cannot be written more rapidly, for the legible forms possible only in vertical writing are more advantageous to speed than the easy movement in slant writing. I believe that vertical writing can be written more rapidly than the standard slant writing.

6. *About what is the slant of the writing you are now employing?*

Ans. The writing I am now employing is vertical.

7. *Should writing which slants only five degrees from the perpendicular be denominated* slant *or* vertical?

Ans. If writing slants only five degrees, it should be denominated vertical, because the movement used is the same as if purely vertical. It is difficult to maintain a five-degree slant with a movement for slant writing. The movement required to write vertical writing may be modified by position of paper, body, etc., so as to make the production slant fifteen degrees from the vertical; and the movement required to write slant may be so modified by slight effort, as to slant not more than fifteen or twenty degrees. It is sometimes difficult to tell by the appearance of the writing whether the intention was to write vertical or slant; but however this may be, the effort to write the vertical is more certain to produce round and legible writing. It is not difficult to maintain a style almost strictly vertical, but I should not hesitate to call a style that slants only five degrees, vertical both as to form and intention on the part of the writer.

8. *Write a complete letter making application for a position as bookkeeper. In this letter penmanship, arrangement, diction, punctuation and use of capital letters will be considered.*

[For the applicant.]

9. *Examiner will grade penmanship of the answers to above questions at forty per cent.*

THEORY AND PRACTICE OF TEACHING.

ELEMENTARY EDUCATIONAL PSYCHOLOGY.

[Wilkinson.]

1. *In what way does the mind of the child differ from that of the adult?*

Ans. It is undeveloped. It has no store of ideas or knowledge upon which to rely. It depends upon memory and the special senses almost entirely.

The adult mind is developed. It has all its experiences and observations stored up upon which to draw for comparison, generalization, etc. It adds to trained memory, and special senses, disciplined imagination, judgment, and reason.

2. *Show the relation of fatigue, attention, and interest.*

Ans. Interest is the condition into which the mind is brought by pleasure, anticipated profit, curiosity, etc., that enables it to secure attention, the holding of all faculties to the contemplation of a given subject, an easy and even delightful task. But if attention be too severely tasked, or the faculties have been overworked or overloaded for any length of time, attention wanes and interest is lost. Interest begets attention, fatigue destroys or weakens interest.

3. *Outline the functions of sensations.*

Ans. To communicate with the outside world through the body as a channel, thus gaining materials for new ideas; to aid in correcting ideas already formed; to protect both mind and body from neglect, misuse and abuse; the eye, ear, nose, tongue and tactile nerves are the only means by which the mind can secure the known to proceed to the study of the unknown.

4. *Illustrate the apperceptive process.*

Ans. One child, an inexperienced one, sees a horse, and to him it is merely a thing about which he can tell you nothing.

Another, who has seen horses before, can tell you his color, relative size, shape, etc.

A third, who is familiar with and knows horses, can probably tell you in addition whether he is well proportioned, whether he is a trotting-horse, a runner, etc.

The reason the first child sees less than the second and the second less than the third, is difference in previous training. The last mind brings more means of seeing than does the second, the second more than the first. They, by experience, are brought into a position to interpret. To their sensations is added image-making, working from within. The object presented acts on the mind and the mind reacts on the object, and this combination of action and reaction is known as apperception.

5. *Why should the larger muscular movements precede the finer in developing motor control?*

Ans. Because there must be a finer coördination of more numerous nerves and muscles in the latter. The control of the larger movements is less complex, and does not require the nice degree of skill that the finer do. In addition, the larger must be in leash, otherwise their being unregulated will hamper and entirely blanket the finer movements.

6. *Explain the various kinds of control resulting from proper will culture.*

Control of the Body—by which the nerves and muscles are coördinated to the health, protection and well-being of all the physical life.

Control of Special Sensations—by which the will holds the eye, ear, etc., to the contemplation of an object until peculiarities have been observed and knowledge gained of the outside world.

Control of Representative Faculties—by which the memory is held to its task of accurate reporting and imagination to its divine-like power of creative image- and ideal-building.

Control of Reflective Faculties—by which judgment is tempered and reason kept sane and well ordered.

Control of Feelings—by which appetite is subjected to impulse, lower impulses to higher, all to principle, and right habits are formed and persisted in until they become the memory of the will.

7. *Define memory, and show upon what it depends.*

Ans. (*a*) Memory is the recording, retention and restoration of past experiences and ideas.

(*b*) It depends upon the force with which the original impression was made; upon the number of times that the impression has been repeated; upon the degree of mental vigor that prevailed at that time as well as at the time it is attempted to be restored, and in many instances upon the vigor that has prevailed in the interval between the two; upon the similarity, contrast or connection in time or place with other mental experiences.

8. *Explain the difference in methods of testing judgments among children and adults.*

Ans. We require greater accuracy on the part of the child upon intuitive judgments, because they are less complex than deliberative judgments; and we hold him to stricter account for synthetic judging than we do for analytic, because in the former his judgments are the results of new and immediate experiences used for the first time. Should the adult present the synthetic judgment we should hold it of little account, as his judgment must be the expression of judgments previously formed; that is, analytic. During school-life by careful gradation we advance the analytic and deliberative as the tests.

9. *Explain how the acts of knowledge affect the self-activity.*

Ans. Knowledge and self-activity affect each the other by action and reaction. We can only perceive our self-activity by introspection, but becoming acquainted with it, knowing it, within ourselves, we learn to recognize its manifestations outside us. Thus we add to knowledge, which in turn, of necessity, quickens self-activity.

10. *In what way does this subject prepare you for teaching?*

Ans. By giving me the thought and experience of others to aid me; by increasing my own self-activity, and enabling me to see it and understand it in the children with whom I am to come in contact.

THEORY AND PRACTICE.

GENERAL PEDAGOGICS AND METHODS.

[Wilkinson.]

1. *Describe the different classes of intellects, and explain how they are discovered in individual cases.*

Ans. It is assumed that the question refers to the classes of minds which may be determined by "temperaments," which are defined by Ladd as "Any marked type of mental constitution and development which seems due to inherited characteristics of the bodily organisms." They are:

(*a*) *Sanguine:* respiratory and circulatory systems well developed; hair red, eyes blue, skin fair, face animated; lively, excitable; quickly but not deeply roused; feelings generally uppermost.

(*b*) *Choleric:* muscular system well developed; hair and eyes dark, complexion sometimes sallow, face impassive; less quick than sanguine; reactions slower and more enduring; determined, self-reliant, confident; will generally uppermost.

(*c*) *Phlegmatic (or lymphatic):* abdomen large, face round and expressionless, lips thick, body generally disinclined to exertion; mind heavy and torpid, sometimes nearly stupid; patient, self-reliant, slow.

(*d*) *Sentimental:* head large, eyes bright and expressive, figure slender and delicate, motions quick; loves poetry, music and nature; marked indifference to practical affairs of life.

(*e*) *Mixed:* most minds are more or less complex, made up of more or less of these.

2. *Name four things that affect the process and limitations in the act of learning.*

Ans. Heredity or class of the intellect; environments of the child at home and at school; previous intellectual training and discipline; character and training of the teacher.

3. *Discuss the function of reasoning in the act of learning, and show how it establishes principles and laws.*

Ans. Reasoning determines the relation between judgments, and so advancing from the known or well understood, it enunciates principles and laws founded upon the truth of the judgments and percepts and concepts which preceded judgment.

4. *When is an act of learning said to be complete?*

Ans. When the knowledge has become a part of one's self-activity.

5. *What is the teacher's relation to the act of learning?*

Ans. That of guide and inspirer only. The true teacher does not assume to make a subject too easy, by attempting to *learn* for the pupil.

6. *What are the objects of the recitation?*

Ans. To test the pupil's knowledge of the subject in hand; to establish its relation to previous knowledge by classification; to impart confidence, strength and felicity in expressing thought; to prepare for the lesson of the morrow.

7. *How would you discover and seat defectives?*

Ans. (*a*) By careful personal attention and quiet tests, and by inquiry at the homes of the afflicted ones.

(*b*) By seating them in advantageous positions to secure the best light, to receive sound perfectly, etc., according to the defect.

8. *What means do you use for securing the friendship and co-operation of the pupils?*

Ans. By forcing upon them by my daily bearing that I am personally interested in each of them, participating in their pleasures as far as possible as well as in their tasks; by showing them that I am their friend, and by showing in myself and awakening in them a pride in and love for the school, its progress and its honor.

9. *How are the lower activities related to the higher mental activities?*

Ans. They precede them. They are the foundations upon which the others must be builded.

10. *How may the teacher magnify the idea of personal worth in his pupils?*

Ans. By appealing to his proper self-love, his just pride

in himself, his love of approbation from his home-folks, his school-fellows, and the community.

PHYSIOLOGY.

[Spangler.]

1. *Name the function of the liver, the secretions of the liver, its relation to glycogen, and describe its position.*

Ans. (*a*) Secretes the bile, which with pancreatic juice forms an important digestive fluid, and also secretes sugar from the fluids of the portal vein, which is decomposed and disappears in the process of nutrition.

(*b*) Bile and glycogen, which last seems to disappear as grape-sugar during nutrition.

(*c*) Glycogen is a white, amorphous, inodorous powder, forming with water an opalescent milky solution. It is secreted in large quantities from the portal circulation by the liver, and disappears, probably as glucose (grape-sugar) during nutrition. This creation, storage and transmission of glycogen indicates that the liver is more valuable as a nutritive than as a digestive organ.

(*d*) It is a large gland of dark reddish brown color and a soft, friable texture, situated in the upper part of the abdominal cavity, rather more on the right than on the left side, and immediately below the diaphragm, into the concavity of which its upper surface fits, and reaches across the middle line above the pyloric end of the stomach.

2. *Where does the energy of the body come from? Name the energies possible in the human body.*

Ans. (*a*) From the chemical unions which occur in the body, and whenever more stable compounds are formed from less stable ones, in which the constituent atoms were less firmly held together.

(*b*) Vital energy, inherited power, oxidation, fermentation, and the chemical inter-atomic forces generated in forming new compounds.

3. *How is the temperature of the body maintained, and what is the normal temperature?*

Ans. (*a*) By oxidation, by chemical changes in the tissues of the body at rest, by the activity of organs at work, by movements of the body and parts of the body, by friction of the moving blood, by the transformation of mechanical forces and the electrical forces manifested in the muscles and nerves into heat.

(*b*) About 98.5°F.

4. *What are the main differences between air taken in and given out by the lungs?*

Ans. That inspired has little adulteration, and is composed of oxygen, nitrogen, watery vapor, and carbonic dioxide. That expired contains a greater proportion of watery vapor, nitrogen and carbon dioxide, together with gaseous impurities from the blood, and much less oxygen.

5. *What is the history of the oxygen taken in by breathing, to its exhalation?*

Ans. The inhaled oxygen passes through the cell-walls of the lungs by osmosis, and is carried by the blood to the heart, from which it is propelled outward to the various tissues of the body. In the first set of cells the oxidation that is carried on is incomplete, the products of imperfect combustion are carried on to another set, and so on until the final products no longer capable of further oxidation in the body, together with the unused oxygen, which is slight, are carried to the kidneys, lungs and skin for excretion. That which returns to the lungs passes back through the veins into the right side of the heart, where it is picked up by the pulmonary artery and carried by the capillaries to the cell-walls of the lungs again. The gaseous matter passes through into the lung-cells by exosmosis, and is expelled through the trachea by the succeeding movement of expiration by the respiratory organs.

6. *Where are the villi? Describe one, and state their function.*

Ans. (*a*) Projecting from the inner surface of the small intestines.

(*b*) Each villus is from one-fiftieth to one thirty-fifth of an inch in length. Some are conical and rounded, but most are compressed at the base in one diameter. The villus is made up of a single layer of epithelial cells covering a framework of connective tissue. Near the surface is an incomplete layer of plain muscular tissue continuous below and forming the deepest layer of the mucous membrane. In the center of the villus is an offshoot of the lymphatic system, sometimes a single vessel with a closed and dilated end, and sometimes a network formed by two main vessels with cross-branches. Outside the lymphatics and beneath the muscular layer is a close network of blood-vessels.

(*c*) They absorb the fluid products of digestion and empty them into the portal vein.

7. *Name all the ferments that aid in digestion, and state where they are produced.*

Ans. Ptyalin is the chemical ferment found in saliva, which is secreted by the salivary glands of the mouth and buccal cavity.

Pepsin and Rennin—two ferments found in gastric juice, secreted by the gastric glands in the inner (mucous) membrane of the stomach.

Trypsin—the chief ferment in pancreatic juice, secreted by the pancreas, is conducted from that gland by a duct to its union with the biliary duct in the duodenum.

Bile—secreted by the liver, has for a long time been considered a most important digestive juice, but it is very doubtful whether it contains a ferment which is digestive.

Intestinal juices—which are secreted in the small intestine by the glands of Brunner and the crypts of Lieberkuhn, cannot be obtained pure to determine the ferments contained in them.

8. *What are the special senses, and which nerves supply them?*

Ans. Sight, optic; hearing, auditory; taste, gustatory; smell, olfactory; touch, certain nerves of the skin, which enter the papillæ of the true skin and wind up into little knots called *tactile corpuscles.* These nerves are about one-fourth as numerous as are the papillæ, and are more numerous in the finger-tips and palms of the hand.

9. *State the effect of stimulants on the system; e. g., alcohol, morphine, and tobacco.*

Ans. The special effects are too numerous to detail here. But generally speaking as stimulants the nerve-force is first excited, and then comes the narcotic reaction—all three being narcotics—which, in case of poisonous doses of the drug having been taken, produces stupor, coma, or convulsions, and, in sufficient quantity, death. In case of disease, when administered by a physician in emergencies, they are force-generators to tide the system over a crisis, but they are always deleterious when resorted to as force-regulators.

10. *What measures would you adopt to revive a drowned person?*

Ans. Remove all clothing from chest of sufferer; turn him face downward with his forearm under his head to free the nostrils and mouth from water; then turn on back and elevate shoulders on a firm support of clothing, etc.;

pull the tongue forward and hold it so by a cloth or band passed over it and under the chin; produce artificial respiration by grasping his arms above the elbow and drawing them back horizontally and above his head, keeping them so for two seconds; then turn the arms down and press them firmly against the sides for two seconds, repeating these movements 15 to 18 times per minute, continuing the operation for two or three hours if necessary. If some one else is at hand, he should press the lower ribs together simultaneously with the upward movement of the arms. Ammonia or other smelling-salts may be applied to the nostrils, and the limbs rubbed *upward* with hot cloths. Hot and cold water dashed alternately on the chest will assist. Artificial respiration may also be produced by rolling the body alternately from the back to the side, or by raising and depressing the chest, in either case 15 to 18 times per minute. When breathing is recovered, place him in a warm bed in a well-ventilated room.

CONSTITUTION.

[Massey.]

1. *Name the three great compromises of the Constitution, and give provisions of each.*

Ans. (*a*) Compromise as to Representation: The Virginia plan proposed that representation in one branch of the Congress should be divided among the States according to the amount of money each State paid into the national treasury, or according to the number of the free inhabitants of each State. The New Jersey plan proposed simply to amend the Articles of Confederation. Benjamin Franklin and Roger Sherman proposed as a compromise the present plan: the appointment of the members of the House of Representatives among the several States according to population, and their choice by the people direct. In the Senate each State, regardless of population or wealth, was given two members, to be chosen by the legislature of the State.

(*b*) Compromise as to Apportionment: The difficulty then turned upon how to determine population for representation in the House of Representatives. Should slaves be counted? Finally, the "federal ratio," counting the slaves at three-fifths their number, was agreed to. This disappeared with the abolition of slavery.

(*c*) Compromise as to the Slave Trade was made by prohibiting Congress from interfering with the slave trade until 1808.

2. *Give qualifications and disqualifications of Senators.*

Ans. (*a*) A Senator must be 30 years of age, nine years a citizen of the United States, and an inhabitant of the State from which chosen.

(*b*) If he be less than thirty years of age, or his citizenship be less than nine years, or he be not an inhabitant of the State from which chosen, or if the Senate refuse to admit him for cause, or if he should be expelled from the Senate, or if he be appointed to and accept any civil office under the authority of the United States, which shall have been created, or the emoluments thereof increased, during the time for which he was elected, or if he holds any office under the United States, or if he have engaged in insurrection or rebellion against the United States, or given aid or comfort to her enemies, unless amnestied by Congress, he shall be disqualified to sit as Senator.

3. *Give powers of Congress relating to Congress.*

Ans. Congress may change the times and manner which have been prescribed by the States of electing its members, and may change the places of choosing Representatives, but not of Senators. It may by law appoint the day for its assembling. It may adjourn its sessions both as to time and place. It provides for apportionment of Representatives among the States. Each house is the judge of the elections, returns and qualifications of its members, may transact business by the presence of a majority of its members, adjourn for a not greater period than three days without the consent of the other house, compel the attendance of absent members in such manner as it sees fit, determine its rules of procedure, punish members for disorder, by concurrence of two-thirds expel a member, and suppress the publication of such parts of its proceedings as it may deem necessary to be kept secret.

4. *Name ten sole powers of the President.*

Ans. Commander-in-chief of the army and navy of the United States, and of the militia of the several States when called into the service of the United States.

Nominates ambassadors, ministers, consuls, judges of the Supreme Court, etc.

Fills all vacancies which occur during the recess of the Senate.

Convenes both houses, or either of them, on extraordinary occasions.

Has the power to adjourn Congress to such time as he may see proper when the houses cannot agree with respect to the time of adjournment.

Receives ambassadors and other public ministers.

Executes all laws.

Issues commissions to all United States officers.

Grants reprieves and pardons for offenses against the United States, except in cases of impeachment.

Compels the opinions in writing of the principal officers in each of the Executive departments.

5. *What is the extent of the judicial power of the United States?*

Ans. To interpret the Constitution, laws and treaties of the United States; to determine questions of conflict between such and those of the several States; to adjudicate and punish offenses against the United States; to determine legal controversies between two or more States—between citizens of different States—between a State and citizens of another State, but not where the suit is commenced or prosecuted against one of the States by citizens of another State, or by citizens or subjects of a foreign power—between citizens of the same State claiming lands under grants of different States—between a State, or citizens thereof, and foreign States, citizens or subjects—and to controversies to which the United States is a party; to determine all cases affecting ambassadors and other public ministers and consuls, and all cases of admiralty and maritime jurisdiction.

6. *Give ten provisions of the Kansas bill of rights.*

Ans. Inalienability of the equal and natural rights: life, liberty and the pursuit of happiness.

All political power inherent in the people, and free government is founded on their authority and instituted for their equal protection and benefit.

The Legislature may not grant any irrevocable or unalterable special privileges or immunities.

The right of the people to assemble in a peaceable manner, to consult, to instruct representatives, and to petition government for the redress of grievances.

The right of the people to bear arms for defense and security.

Standing army not to be permitted, and the military is subservient to the civil power.

The inviolability of trial by jury.

The prohibition of slavery, and of involuntary servitude except for the punishment of crime of which the party shall have been convicted.

Freedom in religious belief and worship of God.

The prohibition of State church.

Excessive bail cannot be imposed, and all offenses, except capital, in which proof is evident or presumption great, are bailable.

No excessive fine nor cruel or unusual punishment can be imposed.

No religious test or property qualification shall be required for any office of public trust, or to vote at any election.

Habeas corpus shall not be suspended, except when necessary to public safety in time of invasion or rebellion.

7. *Give name of each State officer that is elected biennially.*

Ans. Governor, Lieutenant-Governor, Secretary of State, Auditor, Treasurer, Attorney-General, Superintendent of Public Instruction, and Superintendent of Insurance.

8. *How did our trouble with Chili in 1890-'91 originate? How was it settled?*

Ans. Some American sailors from an American ship in the harbor of Valparaiso were attacked by Chilian citizens, and two or three were killed. In the diplomatic correspondence which followed Chili was very haughty, but when the President sent his ultimatum she apologized.

9. *Describe specifically four diplomatic events in our acquisition of the Hawaiian Islands.*

Ans. A revolution took place in Hawaii, Jan. 14, 1893. A provisional government, engineered and directed by the American minister, was set up until terms of union with the United States could be settled. A treaty was negotiated and sent to the United States Senate, but was not acted on while Harrison was President. March 6, President Cleveland withdrew the treaty and sent a commissioner to Hawaii to investigate and report. This commissioner declared the protectorate ended, and lowered the United States flag. Then a new minister was sent to the islands, with instructions, if possible, to reinstate the deposed queen. Late in the year Congress asked the President for information and papers, which he sent, leaving affairs in the hands of Congress. July 4, 1894, a Hawaiian Republic was proclaimed, with Sanford B. Dole as president. In 1897 a new treaty was negotiated with the United States, accepted by President McKinley, sent to the Senate, but not acted on by that body. July 6, 1898, Congress by joint resolution annexed the republic, and the United States flag was raised August 16, 1898. The islands were placed under territorial government, by act of Congress, April 30, 1900.

10. *What motives prompted the United States government to establish the republic of Liberia?*

Ans. Liberia was established in 1820 by the American Colonization Society to provide for the colonization of the negroes of the United States by a gradual process of emigration and settlement. The constitution was modeled after the Constitution of the United States, except it was thus far in advance of our government in recognizing all men free and equal.

PHYSICS.

[Spangler.]

1. *What is force? How is it measured?*

Ans. (*a*) That which causes any change in the form or condition of matter.

(*b*) By the resistance which it can overcome. The unit adopted in this country is that required to overcome the resistance of gravity in moving one pound through a vertical distance of one foot.

2. *What do you understand by the conservation of energy? Illustrate.*

Ans. (*a*) The transformation of one form of energy into another form; as changing heat into electricity, electricity into heat, etc.

(*b*) A wagon going down hill is arrested by the muscular energy of the horses and the friction of the wheels with the ground and of the brake upon the wheels, thus converting the force of gravity and the opposing forces of muscular power and friction into heat.

3. *Explain the action of the siphon.*

Ans. The siphon consists of a bent tube with two unequal arms, and is used to transfer liquids from a higher to a lower level. The shorter arm of the siphon is plunged into the liquid to be transferred, and the action is commenced by removing the air from the longer arm by suction. The water, obeying the pressure of the atmosphere on its surface, rushes in to fill the vacuum thus created. After suction is discontinued, the liquid is pressed up the shorter arm by the weight of the air on the surface of the liquid minus the weight of the water in the shorter arm. At the same time the atmosphere presses up in the long arm of the tube minus the weight of water in the long arm. Hence the water will flow out of the long arm with a flow equal to the difference between the weights of the columns of water in the two arms. The greater the difference between the two arms, the greater will be the velocity of the flow.

4. *What is meant by specific heat? 50 grams of aluminum heated to a temperature of 237° C. are plunged into 100 grams of water at 16° C. The metal having cooled, the temperature of the water is found to be 37° C. What is the specific heat of the aluminum?*

Ans. (*a*) The amount of heat in a body when compared with that contained in the standard, or the heat required to raise one pound of any substance 1° F. compared with the thermal unit. Thus, water is the standard and its specific heat is 1. Now, if different bodies of the same weight be heated to the same temperature (say 212° F.) and then placed on cakes of ice, the amount of ice melted will be in proportion to the number of thermal units they contain; thus in comparison with water, sulphur will melt one-fifth, iron one-ninth, mercury one-thirtieth as much ice, and the specific heats will be: water 1, sulphur .2, iron .111+, mercury .033+.

(*b*) If 50 g. aluminum at 237° raise 100 g. water from 16° to 37°, or 21°, then they would raise 50 g. water twice as many degrees, or 42°, or from 16° to 58°. In doing so the aluminum parts with 179° of heat; therefore its 179° have been consumed in raising the same weight of water 42°, and its specific heat is $\frac{42}{179}$ that of water, or .23+.

5. *How can we measure the velocity of sound?*

Ans. By noting the difference between the time of the

flash of a gun and that at which the report reaches the ear of the observer. Light travels practically instantaneously, hence the time interval must have been consumed by the sound-wave in traveling the distance from the gun to the ear. Measure this distance in feet and divide the number obtained by the number of seconds that elapsed, and the result will be the velocity in feet per second. Then, taking this velocity as the standard for atmosphere at the same density and temperature, the distance of source of any sound can be determined by multiplying this quotient by the number of seconds which elapse between the production of the sound and its reaching the ear.

6. *Give the distinctive features of the incandescent and the arc lamps.*

Ans. In the arc light the wire conducting the current is broken and a carbon pencil is attached to each portion of the wire at the break. The free ends of these pencils are then brought together and then slowly separated, whereupon a brilliant arc of light will continuously play from one pencil to the other unless they are too widely separated.

In the incandescent light a thin film of carbon or platinum is inserted in the break and inclosed in a vacuum within a glass bulb. The resistance offered by the film to the current of electricity generates heat, which causes the film to glow with a white heat and emit light.

7. *What is the critical angle of a substance (light)?*

Ans. The limiting angle of incidence which separates the totally reflected rays from those which (at least partially) escape into the air.

8. *Explain the action of the Leyden jar.*

Ans. The positive spark passes to the interior of the jar. The molecules of the glass are all polarized. Connecting the outer coating of the jar with the ground, the positive electricity escapes, but the outside is charged by induction—the negative being held by the attraction of the positive within the jar. Now, if equilibrium is restored through the human body by touching the inner coating and the outer at the same instant, a distinct shock will be felt.

BOOKKEEPING.

[Bushey.]

August 1. Began business with $1000 cash. Bought merchandise for cash, $350.

Aug. 2. Bought merchandise, and gave note at 6 per cent., $400.

Aug. 5. Sold Brown merchandise, on account, $40. Bought merchandise of Smith, on account, $250.

Aug. 10. Cash sales of merchandise, $180.

Aug. 13. Drew a draft on Brown, favor Smith, $40; gave Smith my note for $110, and cash, $50.

Aug. 15. Bought merchandise of Black, on account, $300. Cash sales, $160.

Aug. 17. Discounted my note of 2d inst. Discount allowed, $4; interest due, $1; paid cash, $397. Merchandise on hand, $950.

Journalize, post, and make statement showing gains and losses, resources and liabilities.

	Debit		Credit
August 1.			
Cash	$1000		
James Forney			$1000
Mdse.	350		
Cash			350
2			
Mdse.	400		
Bills payable			400
5			
Brown	40		
Mdse.			40
Mdse.	250		
Smith			250
10			
Cash	180		
Mdse.			180
13			
Smith	40		
Brown			40
Smith	160		
Cash			50
Bills payable			110
15			
Mdse.	300		
Black			300
Cash	160		
Mdse.			160
17			
Bills payable	400		
Interest	1		
Cash			397
Discount			4

James Forney, proprietor.

Aug.	*17*	*Net capital*		*$1033*	Aug.	1			$1000
					Aug.	17	Gain		33
				$1033					$1033

Cash.

Aug.	1			$1000	Aug.	1			$350
Aug.	10			180	Aug.	13			50
Aug.	15			160	Aug.	17			397

Merchandise.

Aug.	1		$350	Aug.	5		$40
Aug.	2		400	Aug.	10		180
Aug.	5		250	Aug.	15		160
Aug.	15		300	*Aug.*	*17*	*Inventory* ...	*950*
Aug.	*17*	*Gain*........	*30*				
			$1330				$1330

Brown.

Aug.	5		$40	Aug.	13		$40

Smith.

Aug.	13		$40	Aug.	5		$250
Aug.	13		160				

Black.

				Aug.	15		$300

Bills payable.

Aug.	17		$400	Aug.	2		$400
				Aug.	13		110

Interest and discount.

Aug.	17		$1	Aug.	17		$4
Aug.	*17*	*Gain*	*3*				
			$4				$4

Loss and gain.

Aug.	*17*	*James Forney*....	*$33*	Aug.	17	Mdse........	$30
				Aug.	17	Int. and disc.	3
			$33				$33

Trial Balance and Statement.

			Losses.	Gains.	Resources.	Liabilities.
James Forney		$1000				
Cash	$1340	797			$543	
Mdse.................	1300	380		$30	*950*	
Smith	200	250				$50
Black		300				300
Bills payable	400	510				110
Interest and discount.	1	4		3		
	$3241	$3241		$33	$1493	$460
Net gain			*$33*			
			$33	$33		
James Forney, credit.		$1000				
James Forney, gain...		33				
Net capital						*1033*
					$1493	$1493

Saturday, October 26, 1901.

ARITHMETIC.*

[Nichols.]

1. *Simplify the following, and then reduce to a decimal, carrying to four places:*

$$\frac{\frac{2}{3}+3\frac{1}{2}}{1\frac{7}{8}-\frac{5}{12}}$$

Ans.
$$\frac{\frac{2}{3}+3\frac{1}{2}}{1\frac{7}{8}-\frac{5}{12}}=\frac{16+84}{45+10}=\frac{100}{35}=2\tfrac{6}{7}=2.8571+$$

Note.—Multiply both terms of the fraction by 24, the L. C. M. of the small denominators, before performing the other operations.

2. *Reduce five-sevenths ton to lower denominations.*

Ans. $\frac{5}{7}$ T. $=\frac{5}{7}\times 20$ cwt. $=14\frac{2}{7}$ cwt.
$\frac{2}{7}$ cwt. $=\frac{2}{7}\times 100$ lbs. $=28\frac{4}{7}$ lbs.
$\frac{4}{7}$ lbs. $=\frac{4}{7}\times 16$ oz. $=9\frac{1}{7}$ oz.
$\frac{1}{7}$ oz. $=\frac{1}{7}\times 16$ dr. $=2\frac{2}{7}$ dr.
$\therefore \frac{5}{7}$ T. $=14$ cwt. 28 lbs. 9 oz. $2\frac{2}{7}$ dr.

3. *Find the cost of papering the walls and ceiling of a room 9 feet by 12 feet and 10 feet high with paper one-half yard wide, at 20 cents per roll of 24 feet, no allowance being made for doors or windows or for matching.*

Ans. Perimeter of room = 42 ft. No. strips on sides = $\frac{42}{1\frac{1}{2}}=28$. One roll will make two strips, as pieces of strips are not used. No. rolls for sides = $\frac{28}{2}$, or 14. The more economical way is to run the ceiling strips lengthwise of the room. No. strips on the ceiling = 6. No. rolls on the ceiling = $\frac{6}{2}=3$. No. rolls required = 17.
Cost = 17×20¢ = $3.40.

***Answers by E. L. Payne, Emporia, Kan.**

4. *Find the present worth of a note for $8500 due in three months; interest at 8 per cent.*

Ans. 100% P. = present worth.
2% P. = true discount.
102% P. = face of note.
∴ 102% P. = $8500.

$$P. = \frac{\$8500}{1.02} = \$8333\tfrac{1}{3}$$

5. *How many bushels of wheat can be placed, without heaping, in a bin 8 feet by 10 feet by 5 feet.*

Ans. No. bushels $= \frac{8 \times 10 \times 5 \times 1728}{2150.4} = 321.4+$

6. *After marking a certain piece of goods a dealer throws off 10 per cent. If a purchaser who receives an added discount of 4 per cent. for cash pays $21.60 for the piece, what was the first marked price?*

Ans. 96% of discounted price = $21.60.

Discounted price $= \frac{\$21.60}{.96} = \$22.50$.

90% of marked price = $22.50.

Marked price $= \frac{\$22.50}{.9} = \$25$.

7. *What are the names of the three tables of weight? State for what kind of goods each is made. Which weight is the same in all tables? Reduce one ounce avoirdupois to troy weight.*

Ans. Avoirdupois, Troy, and Apothecaries'.

Avoirdupois weight is used in weighing ordinary articles, as grains, fruits, vegetables, coal, etc.

Troy weight is used in weighing precious metals and precious stones.

Apothecaries' weight is used in weighing medicines.

The grain is the same in all.

One oz. Avoir. = 437½ gr. = 18 pwt. 5½ gr.

8. *Find the interest at 6 per cent. on $3765 from June 9, 1897, to August 4, 1898.*

Ans. Subtracting dates we have,
Time = 1 yr. 1 mo. 25 days.

.06
.005
.004⅙
$.069⅙ = interest on $1.

The interest on $3765 is 3765 times $.069⅙, or $260.41+

9. *What is the length of a side of a square 20-acre field? Carry the result to three decimal places.*

Ans. No. sq. rds. $= 20 \times 160 = 3200.$

No. rds. on a side $= \sqrt{3200}.$

$= 56.568 +.$

10. *A woolen manufacturer sends his agent $2100 to invest in wool after deducting 5 per cent. commission. What is the purchase-price and what the commission?*

Ans. 100% P. = purchase price.

5% P. = commission.

105% P. = cost.

∴ 105% P. = $2100.

$\text{P.} = \frac{\$2100}{1.05} = \$2000.$

Commission = $100.

GRAMMAR.

[Bushey.]

(1) *"When all was over, Wellington said*
(2) *to Blucher, as he stood by him on a little*
(3) *eminence looking down upon the*
(4) *field covered with the dead and dying,*
(5) *'A great victory is the saddest thing*
(6) *on earth except a great defeat.'"*

1. *Point out the principal clause in above sentence.*

Ans. "Wellington said to Blucher."

2. *Give construction of "as," line 2.*

Ans. Conj. adverb connecting the clause "as . . .dying" (in 2d, 3d and 4th lines) to the principal clause and modifying the verb "stood" in the subordinate clause.

3. *Give construction of "dying," line 4.*

Ans. Present active participle used as a noun. In the objective case, and is one member of the compound object of the preposition "with."

4. *Give construction of "over," line 1.*

Ans. Adverb, modifying "was."

5. *Give construction of the clause "A great victory," etc., lines 5 and 6.*

Ans. Object of "said," in line 1.

6. *Name the different classes of conjunctions and construct a sentence illustrating each.*

Ans. Conjunctions are divided into two general classes, Coördinate and Subordinate.

(*a*) Coördinate Conjunctions are:
Copulative — He sang *and* she danced.
Adversative — He fell *but* he will rise again.
Alternative — He will go *or* I shall die.
Illative — He goes, *therefore* I remain.

(*b*) Subordinate Conjunctions are:
Causal — He goes *that* you may stay.
Temporal — I shall go *when* you return.
Local — I go *where* I am sent.
Manner or Degree — I know not *how* it happened.

Coördinate or subordinate conjunctions used in pairs, one referring to or answering the other, are called correlatives — He is *both* learned *and* wise.

7. *Write the singular and plural of the following: German, penny, pea, phenomenon, politics, foci, errata, chrysalis, index, knight templar.*

	Singular.	*Plural.*
Ans.	German.	Germans.
	Penny.	Pennies, pence.
	Pea.	Peas, pease.
	Phenomenon.	Phenomena.
	Politics.	(No plural form.)
	Focus.	Focuses or foci.
	Erratum.	Errata.
	Chrysalis.	Chrysalides.
	Index.	Indexes, indices.
	Knight Templar.	Knights Templar.

8. *Give construction of the noun in the following sentence: "They thought him a detective."*

Ans. Harvey, page 183, remark 5, calls this expression the abridged form of an objective clause. He would understand "to be" and modify "him" by the infinitive phrase "(to be) a detective." In such a construction, "detective" is in the objective case, predicate of "him" after "to be" understood.

Maxwell, Advanced Lessons in English Grammar, §§ 527 and 528, calls "detective" a supplement, making it modify the meaning of "him" as an appositive, and supplement the meaning of the verb "thought."

Milne, An English Grammar, note 2, page 298, makes "detective" a secondary object.

Smith, English Grammar, remark 2, page 129, says: "In the sentence 'They elected him captain,' *him* is the object of *elected* and *captain* is the 'factitive object,' *i. e.*, an adverbial modifier denoting the result of the act expressed by the verb. The infinitive *to be* is not understood before captain."

Hoenshel, Complete English Grammar, page 243, says: "'To be' may be supplied before the last object, making the first object the subject of the infinitive and the second object the objective attribute."

Still other authorities designate the construction as "object complement," "objective predicate," etc.

9. *Write a sentence containing a clause used as the object of a preposition.*

Ans. I call your attention to *how matters stand.*

10. *Give a synopsis of the verb* "stand" *in the third person, singular, passive, indicative.*

Ans.

Pres., Is stood.	*Pres. Perf.*, Has been stood.
Past, Was stood.	*Past Perf.*, Had been stood.
Future, Will be stood.	*Fut. Perf.*, Will have been stood.

GEOGRAPHY.

[Nelson.]

1. (a) *Name and locate important rivers in Kansas;* (b) *name chief industries of the State.*

Ans. (*a*) Arkansas—southwest and south-central; Neosho—southeastern; Kansas—east third, north of center; Blue—north, northeast of center; Republican—northwestern and northeast of center; Smoky Hill—western two-thirds, just north of center; Solomon and Saline—little more than western half, north of center, between the Republican and Smoky Hill; Cimarron—extreme southwest; Missouri—along northeastern border.

(*b*) Growth of corn, wheat, potatoes and fruits; milling corn and wheat; grazing and raising live-stock; packing; mining lead, zinc, coal, salt, etc.

2. ***Define isthmus, island, continent, strait, and give example of each.***

Ans. (*a*) Strip of land uniting two larger bodies of land: Isthmus of Panama, connecting North and South America.

(*b*) Body of land entirely surrounded by water: Porto Rico.

(*c*) One of the large bodies or grand divisions of land on the earth's surface: North America.

(*d*) A narrow channel of water connecting two larger bodies of water: Behring strait, connecting the Behring sea and the Arctic ocean.

3. ***What natural causes contribute to the growth of*** (a) ***Kansas City,*** (b) ***San Francisco,*** (c) ***Chicago,*** (d) ***St. Louis,*** (e) ***New York, and*** (f) ***London? Explain fully.***

Ans. (*a*) At the confluence of Kansas and Missouri rivers, it is the gateway to the plains on the west and the States to the east of the Missouri.

(*b*) Seaport of the Pacific coast, because of its fine harbor.

(*c*) Its location on the Great Lakes, with a large tributary farming, grazing, and timber country.

(*d*) The river trade of the Mississippi and Missouri rivers.

(*e*) The metropolis of United States, its fine harbor fronting Europe and its commerce, and outlet for commerce of America toward the east.

(*f*) Position on tidal river; oldest and capital city of British Empire.

4. ***What effect would the Isthmian Canal have upon the*** Australia, Asia, and the islands of the Pacific, and by supplying the cheaper mode of transportation by water.

Ans. Increase it wonderfully, by shortening the distance between our eastern seaboard and great cities and the commercial countries of the Pacific, including eastern Africa, Australia, Asia, and the islands of the Pacific, and supplying the cheaper mode of transportation by water.

5. ***Give chief products of France, Russia, China, Cuba, and Alaska.***

Ans. *France*—Silk, wine, perfumeries, fancy goods.

Russia—Oats, wheat, iron, gold, platinum, silver, furs.

China—Rice, cotton, tea, silk, camphor, opium, sugar.

Cuba—Tobacco, sugar.

Alaska—Gold, furs.

6. *Name and locate four important rivers in the United States, three in Europe, two in South America, and three in Asia.*

Ans. United States: ***Mississippi–Missouri***, central, flows north to south; ***Columbia***, northwest, westerly; ***Colorado***, southwest, southwesterly; ***Rio Grande***, southwest, southeasterly.

Europe: ***Volga***, eastern, southerly; Danube, south-central, easterly; ***Rhine***, western, northerly.

South America: ***Orinoco***, northern, northeast; ***Amazon***, northern, easterly.

Asia: ***Obi***, northern, northerly; ***Yang-tse-Kiang***, southeastern, easterly; ***Indus***, southwestern, southerly.

7. *Define latitude, zone, republic, monarchy, ocean current, and glacier.*

Ans. (*a*) Distance north and south of the equator.

(*b*) A belt of land and water lying between two circles drawn about the earth.

(*c*) A form of government administered by representatives chosen by the people.

(*d*) A form of government administered by one person as sovereign.

(*e*) River of water flowing among the surrounding waters of the sea.

(*f*) A body of ice slowly moving down a slope or incline of land.

8. *Locate Rome, Havana, Berlin, Stockholm, Corsica, Cyprus, Iceland, Alexandria, and Crimea.*

Ans. (*a*) Western Italy, on the Tiber river; capital of Italy.

(*b*) Coast of northwestern Cuba; capital.

(*c*) East-central Prussia; capital of German Empire.

(*d*) Southeastern coast of Sweden; capital.

(*e*) Island north of Sardinia, in Mediterranean sea.

(*f*) Island in the eastern end of the Mediterranean sea.

(*g*) Island in the Atlantic, west of Norway, just south of the Arctic Circle.

(*h*) City of northern Egypt, on the Nile.

(*i*) Peninsula projecting from southern Russia into the Black sea.

UNITED STATES HISTORY.

[Riggs.]

1. *Give an account of the efforts of the French to found a colony in Florida.*

Ans. Ribault explored the coasts of Carolina in 1562. Sailing southward from Carolina, he came to a beautiful river, which he named River of May. It is now called the St. Johns. Ribault left a few men on the coast, and returned to France. But after a year or more these men left, and after fearful hardships reached Europe. In 1565, a large expedition came from France and planted a new colony on the May. After their food was exhausted some of them rebelled, seized a vessel, sailed away to plunder the Spaniards in the West Indies, and told the Spaniards of the colony they had left. The Spaniards under Menendez surprised the colonists and massacred them, and also slaughtered Ribault and his crews that had been shipwrecked at St. Augustine. Although Gourges afterwards with 200 men took St. Augustine and avenged the slaughter by killing its garrison of Spaniards, the French made no more attempts to settle in Florida or the Carolinas.

2. *Name three important battles of the Revolution that were fought in New Jersey.*

Ans. Trenton, Princeton, and Monmouth.

3. *Name four individuals, each in a different department of literary work, who have greatly contributed to the fame of American literature.*

Ans. Benjamin Franklin, autobiography; Nathaniel Hawthorne, fiction; Henry W. Longfellow, poetry; Daniel Webster, oratory.

4. *What were the "X Y Z papers"?*

Ans. In 1797, President Adams sent John Marshall and Elbridge Gerry to coöperate with General Pinckney, our minister to France, for the purpose of avoiding a threatened war with that country. When they reached Paris three men came to them and said that, to avoid difficulty the United States must: (*a*) apologize; (*b*) lend France money; (*c*) bribe the French Directory and its minister of foreign affairs. These outrageous demands were emphatically put aside. In reporting the matter to Congress, the President suppressed the names of the three French agents, calling them "Mr. X, Mr. Y, and Mr. Z," from which fact the papers bearing upon the affair were called the "X Y Z papers."

5. *What was the fugitive-slave law?*

Ans. The most stringent of the fugitive-slave laws was the one passed as a result of the Compromise of 1850. It provided:

(*a*) That United States Commissioners should have the power to turn over a negro man or woman to anyone who claimed the negro as an escaped slave.

(*b*) That the negro could not testify.

(*c*) That all good citizens when summoned should aid in the capture, and in the delivery, if necessary, of a slave to his master.

(*d*) Fines and imprisonment for anybody who harbored a fugitive slave or prevented his recapture.

6. *Give the authority and the occasion of each of the following statements or expressions: "With malice toward none, with charity for all"; "Let us have peace"; "I regret that I have but one life to give for my country"; "We are one nation to-day and thirteen to-morrow"; "We have met the enemy and they are ours."*

Ans. (*a*) Abraham Lincoln, in his second inaugural address, 1865.

(*b*) Ulysses S. Grant, in his letter accepting the nomination of the Republican party for the presidency in 1868.

(*c*) Nathan Hale, before being executed as a spy during the Revolution.

(*d*) George Washington, in speaking of the weakness of the country under the Articles of Confederation, when he, Franklin and others were working for a new Constitution.

(*e*) Oliver H. Perry, in his dispatch reporting the signal victory on Lake Erie.

7. *Name four generals who had command of the army of the Potomac during the Civil War.*

Ans. George B. McClellan, Ambrose E. Burnside, Joseph Hooker, George G. Meade.

8. *When did the Territorial Government of Kansas begin?*

Ans. In 1854.

9. *Who was the first Territorial Governor of Kansas?*

Ans. Andrew H. Reeder.

10. *When and where did the first Territorial Legislature of Kansas meet?*

Ans. At Pawnee, near Fort Riley, July 2, 1855.

READING.

[Massey.]

1. *Define five technical terms used in teaching reading.*

Ans. (*a*) *Gesture*—Any movement of the hands, head, feet, or body intended to assist in interpreting the thought.

(*b*) *Movement*—The degree of rapidity of utterance.

(*c*) *Quality*—The characteristic of the voice caused by the location of resonance; as chest, throat, mouth, etc.

(*d*) *Pitch*—The place on the musical scale assumed by the voice.

(*e*) *Emphasis*—Particular stress thrown upon a certain word or phrase to call attention to it.

2. (a) *Distinguish clearly between the "thought getting" and the "thought expressing."* (b) *What part of the recitation should be given to each?*

Ans. (*a*) "Thought getting" is mastering the thought, making it a part of one's self. "Thought expressing" is conveying that thought to another, by written or spoken speech, or gesture.

(*b*) Such portion of the recitation as may be necessary to enable the child to get the thought, interpret for himself, must be devoted to the preparation of the lesson. The two are of equal importance; for reading has a two-fold object,— to get thought, and to express thought. The pupil cannot express until he clearly understands the thought. So, whatever time is necessary must be given to "thought getting" before attempting to express, that is, read, thought.

3. *What do you mean by the ear vocabulary of the child? Why should his first work in reading be confined to that vocabulary?*

Ans. (*a*) That which comes to him through the sense of hearing, which he has learned by hearing it from the lips of parents, teachers and others.

(*b*) In order that he may give words their right names and pronounce correctly.

4 and 5. *Law: That recitation in reading that fails to*

bring the conscious experience of the child into the lesson is a failure. Take some familiar selection, and in ten concise questions illustrate the law.

Ans. Selection: "THE CATS AND THE MONKEY."

1. What is a fable?
2. Did the cats and monkey talk as they are represented as doing?
3. Give a description of a cat.
4. Tell how a monkey looks and acts.
5. What is a balance, and how did the monkey use this one?
6. How did the cats first get the cheese?
7. The monkey was judge. What were the cats?
8. When the cats were satisfied, why did the monkey not do as they wished?
9. Was his reason a good one, and do you consider him honest?
10. What moral does this fable teach?

ORTHOGRAPHY.

[Riggs.]

1. *Define monosyllable, primitive, derivative, articulation, enunciation, pronunciation.*

Ans. (*a*) A word of one syllable.

(*b*) A word from which other words are derived.

(*c*) A word derived from another word.

(*d*) Utterance of elementary sounds by appropriate movements of the organs of speech.

(*e*) Mode of utterance or pronunciation, especially as regards fullness and distinctness of enunciation.

(*f*) The act of giving the proper sound and accent to a word.

2. *Analyze the words defined in question 1.*

Ans. *Monosyllable*—Latin, monosyllabus.

Primitive—Latin, primitivus, from primus, the first.

Derivative—Latin, derivativus, from derivare, de (from) + rivus (stream).

Articulation—Latin, articulatio.

Enunciation—Latin, enuntiatio.

Pronunciation—Latin, pronunciatio.

In the second and third the English suffix *ive*, signifying relating to, belonging to, or concerning, has been added to the original Latin word.

In the last three the English suffix *ion*, signifying act, process, state, or condition, has been added to the original Latin word.

In the first, the Latin word is made up of two Greek words meaning *one* and *syllable*.

3-10. *Spell: Releef, ocupant, intence, eligible, admitence, curteus, simpathyse, arraign, mannidgement, exentrick, perrilus, comershal, preseeded, exelent, persute, imence, parrimount, hospittle, ballence, plateau, annalize, millionare, catarrh, avalable.*

[See any dictionary.—Ed.]

PENMANSHIP.

(Wilkinson.)

What should be the position when writing vertical hand?

Ans. The position that conduces most to the verticality of the vertical hand is that of the straight front position of the body, with the paper straight in front of the writer; *i. e.*, inclining neither to the left nor right. The front position of the body should be maintained for all kinds of writing, the difference being only in the position of the paper. The paper should slant—lie with the right forearm—when writing the slant hand. By maintaining the position of the body and the movement used in slant, and gradually changing the paper to a straight-in-front position, it will be noticed that the writing becomes more and more upright, until, when the paper reaches the vertical position, the writing will be vertical.

It will be observed at this point that the movement rightward has become somewhat locked and there is not that smoothness that there is when the paper is straight with the arm. But there is not as much objection to this as appears at first sight, because the writing can be done rapidly and legibly in this way; and these are the essential features of a good hand. This way of writing may necessitate a kind of whole-arm movement or an occasional lifting of the pen in the writing of long words; but neither of these is objectionable so long as the results can be obtained easily.

For those desiring to write with the muscular movement

it might be well to compromise as to the position of the paper, and take advantage of a little smoother movement, although the direction of the strokes to secure the vertical might not be so much in line, with the natural movement of the hand and arm. Whatever slight inconvenience there may be experienced as to the movement in securing the vertical hand, it is more than balanced by the confidence with which the writer may execute his work, as to legibility, and by the greater ease with which the reader may see the words and read the page.

THEORY AND PRACTICE.

ELEMENTARY EDUCATIONAL PSYCHOLOGY.

[Wilkinson.]

1. *How would you teach your pupils to find and to remember values of metric units in terms of common measures?*

Ans. This would be in the nature of an object lesson. They should be provided with standards of both systems, and should be required, in addition to memorizing the tables in each system and the equivalents in the other system, to actually measure the same dimensions and quantities in the units of each system, and to note the results.

2. *Would you give work in school for the training of the memory without seeking any other good result? Reasons for your answer.*

Ans. In extreme cases, yes. Where the memory is lamentably deficient, or the mind is easily confused by attempting to do too much at once. Generally, however, the development of the faculties should be carried forward harmoniously, and each task assigned should embrace the exercise of as many faculties as possible. In addition, the act of memory itself is strengthened by exciting the interest and enlisting the attention because of some good, practical, or useful object shown to be contemplated.

3. *Mention two common defects resulting from heredity, and two from environment, and state what you would do to remove them.*

Ans. (*a*) Heredity:

Mental.—The defect of sanguine temperament can only

be remedied by carefully establishing habits of steady and continuous work; the pupil of callous disposition must be developed by awakening and constantly appealing to his sympathetic instincts; the excitable disposition requires constant care in bringing into control his dormant prudential instincts; the energetic must be taught lessons of politeness, good breeding and refinement; while to the sluggish one must be presented such lessons of the moralities and virtues as will appeal to his moral instincts.

Physical.—Abberation of sight, defect in hearing, etc., remedied or ameliorated by giving the most advantageous positions in seats and at class for the peculiar weakness; by giving lessons in the care of the organs, cleanliness, light, heat, etc., etc.

(*b*) Environment:

Insufficient clothes and books.—If parents cannot afford proper quantity and quality of both, judicious, very judicious measures, should be resorted to to have either the public or private individuals to supply them.

Home Surroundings not Good.—Visit the pupil. Have the pupil visit the teacher. Encourage other desirable companions among the pupils to associate with the afflicted one. If possible, have a talk with parents and secure their coöperation in bettering home conditions.

4. *Would you give work in school for the training in habit, without seeking any other good result? Reasons for your answer.*

Ans. No. Because the habit if of no good use to the child is actually detrimental. It is a sad loss of time and effort to require the doing of anything with nothing good in view. It may, however, be said that any habit gives control of the faculties; but if it is not a good control, what is its value?

THEORY AND PRACTICE.

GENERAL PEDAGOGICS AND METHODS.

(Wilkinson.)

1. *How would you teach pupils so as to help them understand the law for falling bodies coming under the influence of gravitation alone?*

Ans. Such teaching must be done by experiment, which is a form of object-lesson work. Drop a bullet and a feather in a vacuum, calling attention to the equal rapidity of descent. Then drop them in the air, showing the opposing force of the buoyancy of the air in retarding the fall of the feather. This shows the gravity to be alike on all bodies. By dropping bullets from various heights, show the greater velocity of the one falling through the greater distance. To measure the rate, permit a round body to move freely down a graduated, smooth inclined plane. Carefully observing the spaces passed over in each successive second, the pupil is led to frame the laws for himself.

2. *What are the subjective, the objective and the absolute limits of education?*

Ans. (*a*) The individuality of the youth. Whatever does not exist in the individuality cannot be developed from it. Education cannot create.

(*b*) The means which can be appropriated for it; the amount of time the student may devote to his training.

(*c*) The time when the youth has apprehended the problem which he has to solve, has learned to know the means at his disposal, and has acquired a certain facility in using them.—*Rosenkranz.*

3. *Describe the fan system of heating and ventilation...*

Ans. In the fan system, a mechanical system of some kind is used,— steam engine, gasoline engine or any other motor to drive fresh air into a building, forcing it over heated pipes if desired, for the purpose of warming it. Fans are also used, sometimes, to draw the foul air out of the building, if the force of the fans driving in fresh air is not sufficient to change the air rapidly enough to keep it pure.

4. *What points would you consider in determining the grade you are to give a pupil on his recitation?*

Ans. The diligence shown in preparing the lesson; the progress indicated by the individual pupil; the interest exhibited in the recitation; the clearness of understanding arrived at; the ease, force and lucidity with which he expresses the thought; the amount of information he has acquired about the lesson. Finally, but by no means last, his native ability, physical condition, and environment are important factors in establishing his grade.

PHYSIOLOGY.

[Spangler.]

1. *State important differences between cartilage and bone—chemical, physical, etc.*

Ans. Cartilage contains less lime than does bone, and is therefore less rigid, and will yield or bend under pressure without breaking. Generally, bones are cartilaginous when first formed, and many cartilages of the body become bony in character with the advance of age. The cartilage contains animal matter in greater proportion than it does mineral matter. The reverse is true of bone.

2. *Name the bones of the arm and leg.*

Ans. *Arm:* Shoulder-bone, or scapula; collar-bone, or clavicle; upper-arm bone, or humerus; fore-arm bones, radius and ulna; eight wrist-bones; nineteen bones of the hand.

Leg: Hip-bone; thigh-bone, or femur; two leg-bones, tibia and fibula; the knee-cap, or patella; seven ankle-bones; nineteen bones of the foot.

3. *How is the body kept warm, and what is its temperature?*

Ans. (*a*) By the chemical processes of digestion; by the disintegration of chemical substances and formation of new compounds; by oxidation of food and tissue in contact with the oxygen carried by the blood.

(*b*) About 98.5° F. In the internal organs, the temperature is higher, about 107° F.

4. *Describe the circulation of the blood.*

Ans. The blood is discharged into the right auricle of the heart by the descending vena cava; thence into the right ventricle; thence through the pulmonary artery to the lungs; there distributed by the capillaries, parting with its carbonic acid gas and other gaseous impurities and receiving oxygen through the lung-cell walls; thence capillaries convey it into the pulmonary vein, which discharges into the left auricle; thence into the left ventricle; thence through the aorta, which branches and subdivides again and again until the capillaries bring it to every tissue of the body; here the blood receives new supplies of carbonic acid gas, and leaves its nutritive properties behind; it is then picked up by the capillaries, conveyed into the veins, and at last is emptied into the descending vena cava, to again begin its circuit from the right auricle of the heart.

5. ***What are the excretory organs, and what products do they excrete?***

Ans. (*a*) The lungs and mouth, skin, large intestine, liver, kidney, bladder, probably the spleen.

(*b*) Carbonic acid gas, poisonous substances, substances containing no nutriment, undigested and indigestible matter, and all the waste products of digestion and assimilation.

6. ***State all the principal regions that a piece of bread passes through during digestion.***

Ans. Mouth, œsophagus, stomach, duodenum, small intestine.

7. ***What effect has alcohol on the heart and the temperature of the body?***

Ans. (*a*) Its first effect upon the heart is to increase in force and frequency the heart-beats; this is called stimulation. Then follows the reaction, which diminishes the intensity and rate of contraction and expansion. Its continued use causes the change of muscle cells to fat. On exertion, weakness and fatigue result, causing a need for more stimulation, which spurs on the already tired heart, causing further fatty degeneration.

(*b*) The oxidation of alcohol is so rapid that the system cannot use the heat produced, and expends vital force in attempting to throw off the increased temperature. The sense of warmth it produces being purely deceitful, since it is due to the heat passing from the interior of the body through the capillaries.

8. ***Describe the eye, and uses of the principal parts.***

Ans. (*a*) The eye consists of a round hollow shell about three-fourths of an inch in diameter, formed by a very tough membrane about one-sixteenth of an inch thick, called the sclerotic coat. The sclerotic coat is lined with a thin black membrane, known as the choroid coat, which carries the blood-vessels, and is colored black to prevent reflection of the rays of light. Spread out over the choroid coat is a thin transparent membrane, an extended expansion of the optic nerve, called the retina, to receive the image formed by the refraction of the rays of light. The optic nerve enters the back part of the eyeball and carries the image to the brain. The cavity of the ball is filled in front with a thin clear fluid, the aqueous humor, and in the back with a thick, jelly-like fluid, the vitreous humor. Between and separating these two humors is a lens-shaped membrane, which can be changed at will by the action of muscles, called the crystalline lens. The two humors and the lens serve to refract the rays of light, bringing them to a focus just in front of the retina. The humors also serve to distend the ball and keep it in shape. A prominent transparent tissue, the cornea, forms a round window in the front of the ball, admitting the light. Behind the cornea hangs a curtain, the iris, which gives the color to the eye, and in the center of which is a hole called the pupil. The iris is made up of muscle fibers which can contract and make the pupil smaller, thus regulating the amount of light admitted to the retina.

9. *What are the injurious effects of tobacco, coffee, and tea?*

Ans. (*a*) *Tobacco*—is a poison to the heart's muscles, causing that organ to beat with less strength. In large quantities it poisons the heart's nerves, causing palpitation and inharmonious action. Tobacco-smoke carries the nicotine and other poisons into the lungs, where they are absorbed. It also produces irritation and inflammation of the bronchi, throat, and mouth. Because of the act of smoking, the blood flows to the brain, producing a demand upon the heart, which is already weakened, and cannot meet the demand, causing the brain to act less strongly than before. The nicotine is also a direct poison to the nerve-cells of the brain. Tobacco weakens the optic nerve, causing dimness of vision. The smoke of tobacco irritates the vocal cords and the throat, produces a dry, hacking cough, and husky tones. Excessive use will set up cancer in the mouth and throat.

(*b*) *Tea and Coffee*—are, like alcohol, stimulants; they increase nerve action and excitation, without supplying any energy to carry on the increased action. They are liable to hinder digestion, by the action of the tannin upon albumen. They enable a person to do increased work in an emergency; but used continually, the body relies upon their stimulation.

10. *Describe the organs that take part in respiration; the object of respiration, and how is it attained?*

Ans. (*a*) The abdominal muscles, the intercostal muscles and the diaphragm, by expansion enlarge the capacity of the chest, and by contraction expel the deteriorated air from the lungs. The ribs form the box within which the lungs expand when filled with air. The lungs are made up of masses of air-cells or sacs, connecting with the outside air by means of the tubes which open into the bronchi, which in turn communicate with the trachea.

(*b*) To introduce oxygen into the blood as a result of inhalation, and to expel poisonous vapors and gases by exhalation.

(*c*) The interchange of oxygen for the poisonous gases and vapors is obtained by the action of osmosis through the lung cell-walls, the oxygen passing by endosmosis into the blood in the capillaries of the pulmonary vein, and the poisonous gases and vapors by exosmosis from the pulmonary artery capillaries into the lung cells.

CIVIL GOVERNMENT.

[Massey.]

1. *Give all the provisions of the Constitution as set forth in the preamble.*

Ans. To form a more perfect union, establish justice, insure domestic tranquillity, provide for the common defense, promote the general welfare, and to secure the blessings of liberty to all citizens of the United States for all time.

2. *Name the powers of Congress.*

Ans. To borrow money on the credit of the United States; to establish a uniform rule of naturalization and uniform laws on the subject of bankruptcies; to regulate commerce with foreign nations, among the several States and with the Indian tribes; to coin money, regulate the value thereof, and of foreign coin, and to fix a standard of weights and measures; to establish postoffices and post-roads; to raise and support armies; to provide and maintain navies; to constitute tribunals inferior to the Supreme Court; to declare war, grant letters of marque and reprisal, and make rules concerning captures on land and water; to make all laws necessary and proper to carry all the powers granted to the Government of the United States, or in any department thereof, into execution.

3. *Explain how the Constitution may be amended.*

Ans. 1. Congress may, by two-thirds affirmative vote, propose an amendment, or it shall call a convention to so propose when requested to do so by the legislatures of two-thirds of the several States.

2. When proposed in either of the above ways, the amendment becomes a part of the Constitution, upon being ratified by the legislatures of three-fourths of the several States, or by conventions in three-fourths thereof. But which of the modes of ratification shall be followed is to be determined by Congress.

4. *Distinguish clearly between the duties of ambassador and consul.*

Ans. The ambassador is intrusted with the duty of looking after our relations with the country to which he is accredited. He carries on the diplomatic correspondence, negotiates treaties, represents our government in all political matters. The consul looks after the commercial interests of his country, gathers statistics concerning agriculture, industries, labor, etc., etc., collects duties, and in the first instance protects his countrymen in their rights of property and person while abroad.

5. *Give a brief history of our relations with the Hawaiian Islands.*

Ans. The revolutionists, with the assistance of American marines, deposed the native queen and established a provisional government. This government then negotiated a treaty of annexation to the United States. That treaty while before the Senate for consideration, was recalled by President Cleveland, who sent a commissioner to investigate. Upon this commissioner's report the President hauled down the American flag. The native party was not able to regain control, and in 1898, during the Spanish War, negotiations were reopened for annexation, resulting in Hawaii becoming a portion of United States territory by a joint resolution of Congress.

6. *What is your idea of the best method of dealing with anarchy in America? Be specific.*

Ans. I would forbid the transmission of anarchistic literature through our mails. I would make any anarchist who counseled violence or murder an accessory before the fact to every crime committed against the Government, or any officer thereof, in consonance with such counsel. I would arrest and punish every one who gave such counsel as soon as he gave it, making the penalty severe for the giving of the counsel. I would require every immigrant to this country to bring with him a certificate from our minister or consul to the country from which he comes, showing him to be a supporter of law, order, and government. I would make any attempt upon the life of the President, Vice-President, or any one in the presidential succession, treason, punishable with death. I would restrain the unbridled license, the abuse of free speech, which characterizes presidential campaigns. Finally, I would introduce the teaching of religion and patriotism and obedience and discipline in all our schools, especially in our public schools, and I would continue that as daily compulsory teaching from the cradle to manhood.

PHYSICS.

[Spangler.]

1. *What is the law of hydrostatic pressure?*

Ans. Liquids transmit pressure exerted upon any portion of their mass in all directions, and without sensible loss of intensity. From which it follows that the total pressure sustained by any surface is proportional to its area; that pressure increases with the depth of the liquid and with its density; that upward, downward and lateral pressures at any point within the liquid balance one another.

2. *Describe carefully some method of measuring the velocity of sound.*

Ans. Note the time between the flash of a gun and its report, when fired at a distance from you in a still atmosphere. Divide the distance by the number of seconds that elapse between the flash and the report, and the quotient will be the velocity of sound per second in a still atmosphere having the same density and temperature as that in which the experiment is conducted.

3. *State Ohm's law, and calculate the current from six cells in parallel, the resistance of each cell being two ohms and the outside resistance being eight ohms. The E. M. F. of each cell is one and one-tenth volts. Would a stronger current be obtained by joining the cells in series?*

Ans. (*a*). The current is directly proportional to the

electro-motive force acting on the circuit, and inversely proportional to the resistance of the circuit.

(*b*) $\text{Amperage} = \frac{\text{Voltage}}{\text{Resistance}} = \frac{6\times1.1}{(6\times2)+8} = \frac{6.6}{20} = .33$ ampere.

(*c*) No. The current would be feebler.

4. *If a pendulum whose length is three makes twenty oscillations per minute, how many oscillations by one whose length is four?*

Ans. The duration of the oscillations of two pendulums of different lengths is proportional to the square roots of the lengths.

If a pendulum makes 20 oscillations in a minute, the duration of a single oscillation is 3 seconds.

3 (duration of oscillation of given pendulum) :

x (duration of oscillation of required pendulum) : :

$\sqrt{3}$ (sq. root of length of given pendulum) :

$\sqrt{4}$ (sq. root of length of required pendulum).

$3:x::\sqrt{3}:\sqrt{4}$

$3\sqrt{4}=x\sqrt{3}$

$6=x\sqrt{3}$

$x=\frac{6}{\sqrt{3}}$ or 3.47 nearly, duration of an oscillation of required pendulum. Divide 60 seconds by this duration of an oscillation and the quotient will be the number of oscillations per minute, or 17, about.

5. *What is the difference between quality and loudness of a tone?*

Ans. By intensity of sound is meant that peculiarity which enables us to determine between a loud and a feeble tone. By quality or timbre is meant the characteristic by which we determine whether a sound is made upon a flute, a violin, a piano, by the human voice, etc., and also by which we distinguish one voice from another.

6. *Explain the principle of the barometer.*

Ans. The barometer depends upon the principle of balanced pressures. The column of air pressing upon the surface of mercury in the reservoir supports a column of mercury of equal weight within the tube. Should the air grow lighter, it cannot support so heavy a column of mercury; consequently the mercury falls. Should the air become heavier, the reverse is true.

7. *What is the value of gravitation at the earth's center, and why?*

Ans. Zero. Because the force of gravity attracts matter at the earth's center equally in all directions. These opposing attractions destroy one another.

8. *Explain the action of the carbon telephone.*

Ans. The microphone transmitter for telephonic use consists of a quantity of loose granulated carbon, so placed back of a diaphragm as to vary the electric resistance of a circuit on the movements of the diaphragm by the sound-waves. This produces variations in the current of electricity which flows through the circuit, and these variations reproduce in the receiving telephone the sounds causing them.

BOOKKEEPING.

[Bushey.]

1. *Define:* (a) *Assets,* (b) *resources,* (c) *debtor,* (d) *bills payable,* (e) *discount.*

2. *Make ten day-book entries, containing at least one draft.*

3. *Journalize* (2).

4. *Post* (2).

5. *Rule a cash-book and make proper entries from* (2) *in same.*

6. (a) *Rule a six-column journal.* (b) *What advantage does it possess?*

Ans. 1. (*a*) The entire property of all sorts belonging to a person.

(*b*) Money or property that can be converted into supplies.

(*c*) One who owes.

(*d*) Notes outstanding; our written promises to pay another.

(*e*) An allowance; an amount deducted from a bill.

Oct. 1. Bought bill of goods amounting to $700, paying cash			$700	
2. Sold Geo. H. Collins on acct. mdse. amounting to			162	45
3. Drew a sight draft on G. B. Meech in favor of Brown Bros			200	
4. Received cash of Charles L. Welsh on acct			120	
5. Paid for office books, in cash			35	
6. Sold Geo. W. Carter on account, bill of mdse			193	
7. Bought for cash bill of goods amounting to			345	
8. Sold for cash bill of mdse			196	
9. Bought for cash bill of goods amounting to			320	
10. Paid employe's salary in cash			163	

JOURNAL. October 1, 1901.

	Mdse	$700	
	Cash		$700
	2.		
	Geo. H. Collins	162 45	
	Mdse		162 45
	3.		
	Brown Bros	200	
	G. B. Meech		200
	4.		
	Cash	120	
	Charles L. Welsh		120
	5.		
	Expense	35	
	Cash		35

		6.		
		Geo. W. Carter	193	
		Mdse		193
		7.		
		Mdse	345	
		Cash		345
		8.		
		Cash	196	
		Mdse		196
		9.		
		Mdse	320	
		Cash		320
		10.		
		Expense	163	
		Cash		163

LEDGER.

Merchandise.

Oct.	1			$700	Oct.	2			$162 45
Oct.	7			345	Oct.	6			193
Oct.	9			320	Oct.	8			196

Cash.

Oct.	4			$120	Oct.	1			$700
Oct.	8			196	Oct.	5			35
					Oct.	7			345
					Oct.	9			320
					Oct.	10			163

Brown Bros.

Oct.	3			$200					

G. B. Meech.

					Oct.	3			$200

Charles L. Welsh.

					Oct.	4			$120

Geo. W. Carter.

Oct.	6			$193					

Expense.

Oct.	5			$35					
Oct.	10			163					

Geo. H. Collins.

Oct.	2			$162 45			

CASH BOOK.

DR. *Cash received.*

Oct.	4	Charles L. Welsh.	On acct.	$120	
Oct.	8	Mdse.		196	

Cash paid out. CR.

Oct.	1	Mdse.		$700	
Oct.	5	Expense.		85	
Oct.	7	Mdse.		345	
Oct.	9	Mdse.		320	
Oct.	10	Expense.		163	

No. 6.

Mdse.	*Cash.*	*Sunds.*		*Sunds.*	*Cash.*	*Mdse.*

Possesses advantage of saving posting the separate items entered in the special columns, as the footings only need be posted.